JOKELOPEDIA

JOKELOPEDIA

The Biggest, Best, Silliest, Dumbest Joke Book Ever

✧ ✧ ✧

Compiled by

Ilana Weitzman, Eva Blank, and Rosanne Green

Illustrations by

Mike Wright

WORKMAN PUBLISHING · NEW YORK

Thank yous

☆ ☆ ☆

We wanted this collection of jokes to be the biggest, best, dopiest, silliest, dumbest one on the planet. But that wouldn't have been possible without a lot of help from our friends.

Jill Bryant at Somerville House coordinated the project. Sam McKay helped to get us started. Camilla Dietrich, our humor consultant, sleuthed out super sidebars and gave us valuable feedback. Our comedy team at Colborne Communications included writers Cy Strom and Michael Redhill, and editors Greg Ioannou, Laura Siberry, Suzanne Brandreth, and Vivien Leong who helped us put the whole thing together. Thanks also to Jill Kopelman.

Kids from all over North America sent in some of the coolest jokes in the book and we'd like to thank them. And extra-special thanks to all our joke guinea pigs who had to spend months listening to our worst groaners and stinkiest wisecracks.

Ilana, Rosanne, and Eva
March 2000

Library of Congress Cataloging-in-Publication Data

Jokelopedia : the biggest, best, silliest, dumbest, dopiest joke book ever! / [collected by] Ilana Weitzman, Eva Blank, Rosanne Green.
p. cm.
ISBN-13: 978-0-7611-1214-3
ISBN-10: 0-7611-1214-6 (alk. paper)
1. Wit and humor, Juvenile. 2. Riddles, Juvenile. [1. Jokes. 2. Wit and humor.]
I. Weitzman, Ilana. II. Blank, Eva. III. Green, Rosanne.
PN6163 .J63 2000
818'.60208—dc21   00-044925

Cover Design: Paul Gamarello
Interior Design: Janet Vicario and Natsumi Uda

Workman books are available at special discounts when purchased in bulk for premiums and sales promotions as well as for fund-raising or educational use. Special editions or book excerpts can also be created to specification. For details, contact the Special Sales Director at the address below.

Workman Publishing Company, Inc.
708 Broadway
New York, NY 10003-9555

www.workman.com

Printed in the United States of America

First printing October 2000

20 19 18 17 16 15 14 13

So you want to be funny? Welcome to *Jokelopedia*. We see it as a big, thick reminder of the lighter side of life and hope you use it to make your friends and family groan and smile—although not necessarily in that order.

Do you know what a shaggy-dog joke is? Have you ever seen a chicken cross the road? Well, you will soon. Would you like to make your classmates laugh so hard at lunchtime that milk comes out of their noses? Do you feel like wowing them with humor history from The Three Stooges to *The Simpsons*? Do you want to tell the funniest jokes, learn how your favorite comedians made a living before comedy, how sitcoms came to be, and how to make people laugh, *your* way? If so, this is the book for you.

With contributions from kids, tricky tongue twisters, long long jokes, short short jokes, and general crazy ideas and tips, this just might be the funniest book ever.

No joke.

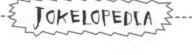

CONTENTS

TALL TAILS
Animals with Attitude

> Did you hear the one about the giraffe?

Did you hear the one about the lion who ate clowns?

You'll roar.

Did you hear the one about the donkey who watched Country Music Television?

You'll hee-haw.

Why shouldn't you shortchange a skunk?

It's bound to make a stink.

What did the judge say when the skunk came in to testify?

Odor in the court!

> Oh, well, it's way over your head.

EAT

There were these two buddies out walking their dogs, one with a Doberman pinscher and the other with a Chihuahua, when they smelled something delicious coming from a nearby restaurant.

The guy with the Doberman says to his friend, "Let's go over to that restaurant and get something to eat." The guy with the Chihuahua says, "We can't go in there. We've got dogs with us."

The buddy with the Doberman says, "Just follow my lead." He puts on a pair of dark glasses and walks into the restaurant, when the restaurant owner comes up and says, "Sorry, pal, no pets allowed."

The man with the Doberman replies, "You don't understand. This is my Seeing Eye dog."

The owner, skeptical, says, "A Doberman pinscher?"

The Doberman's master says, "Yes, they're using them now— they're very good and they protect me from robbers, too." The man at the door says, "Come on in."

When the man with the Chihuahua sees this, he puts on a pair of dark glasses and starts to walk in. Once again the restaurant owner says, "Sorry, pal, no pets allowed."

The guy with the Chihuahua says, "You don't understand. This is my Seeing Eye dog."

"A Chihuahua?" says the owner.

The man with the dog replies, "A Chihuahua? They gave me a Chihuahua?!" ✩

2

ha-ha!

What do you call an overweight cat?

A flabby tabby.

Why was the rabbit so unhappy?

She was having a bad hare day.

What does a chipmunk get when it rains?

It gets wet, silly.

3

THE MAKING OF A COMEDIAN

Step 1: What Is a Joke Made Of?

What makes a joke a joke? What is the difference between the biggest, best, silliest, dumbest, dopiest joke ever and one that falls totally flat?

First is the *setup*. Launch right into the joke. Make sure you know the whole thing backwards and forwards—there's nothing quite as embarrassing as realizing you forgot the funny part.

Next is *timing*. Comedic timing is a skill that takes lots and lots of practice to perfect. Don't rush through your joke. Give your audience time to figure it out. But don't wait too long, or they'll lose interest.

Finally: the *punch line*. This is the last part of a joke—the part you've been building up to, whether you've been telling a long shaggy-dog joke (more on those later!) or a short-'n'-sweet riddle. It's the funny part. Tell it loudly and firmly. Don't laugh in the middle of it, or you ruin the suspense. Leave that up to your audience. The punch line should have an effect like its name—a punch of silliness, right to the funny bone.

The Care and Feeding of King Cobras by I. Will Havastroke.

BOOK TITLES We'd Love to See:

Planning a Surprise Party by Al B. Darn

Are You a Liar? by I.M. Knott

Skydiving by Hope Shue-Topins

World Travel by I.M. Tyred and Jett L'Agg

Crazy Stuff to Do by Ima Loony

Fibbing Effectively by Liza Lott

101 Ways to Miss a Day of School by Ben Barphin

My 1,001 Favorite Chocolate Recipes by Fanny Izlarj

101 Hot 'n' Spicy Meals by Tung Payne

The Art of Shaving by Harry Mann

Rottweiler! by B. Wearuv D'Aug

Hard Math by Jean Yuss

Clean Bathrooms by Ty D. Boal

4

A man walks into a diner carrying a dog under his arm. He puts the dog on the counter and announces that the dog can talk. The man says he has $100 he's willing to bet anyone who says he can't. The head cook quickly takes the bet, and the dog's owner looks at the dog and asks, "What's the thing on top of this building that keeps the rain out?"

The dog answers, "*Roof.*" The cook says, "Who are you kidding? I'm not paying."

The dog's owner says, "Double or nothing, and I'll ask him something else." The cook agrees and the owner turns to his dog and asks, "Who was the greatest baseball player ever?"

The dog answers with a muffled "*Ruth.*"

With that the cook picks them both up and tosses them out on the street. As they bounce on the sidewalk in front of the diner, the dog looks at his owner and says, "DiMaggio?" ☆

Funny Fact

Did you know it takes 17 muscles to smile and 43 to frown?

5

What do you do if your Golden Retriever won't stop sneezing?

Call a dogtor.

A man sitting in a movie theater notices that there is a bear sitting next to him. Finally he turns to the bear and says, "Aren't you a bear?" The bear nods, so the man says, "So what are you doing at the movies?" The bear says, "Well, I liked the book." ☆

A monkey, a bear, a cockatoo, a gerbil, and a rhinoceros all stood under the same umbrella. Who got wet?

Nobody. It wasn't raining, silly.

How did the tree feel after the beaver left?

Gnawed so good.

Knock, knock.
Who's there?
The interrupting cow.
The interrup—
MOOOOOOOOOOOOOO!

One day, a cat died of natural causes and went to heaven. There he met Saint Peter at the Pearly Gates. Saint Peter said to the cat, "You have lived a good life, and if there is any way I can make your stay in heaven more comfortable, please let me know."

The cat thought for a moment and said, "All my life I have lived with a poor family and have had to sleep on a hard wooden floor."

"Say no more," Saint Peter replied, and poof! A wonderful, fluffy pillow appeared.

A few days later, six mice were killed in a tragic farming accident and went to heaven. Again there was Saint Peter to greet them with the same offer. The mice answered, "All of our lives we have been chased. We have had to run from cats, dogs, and even women with brooms. We are tired of running. Do you think we could have roller skates so that we don't have to run anymore?" Instantly each mouse was fitted with a beautiful pair of roller skates.

About a week later, Saint Peter stopped by to see the cat and found him snoozing on the pillow. He gently woke the cat and asked, "How are things for you since coming to heaven?"

The cat stretched, yawned, and replied, "It's wonderful here—even better than I could have expected. Especially those meals-on-wheels you've been sending by—those are the best!" ☆

Where do dogs buy their underwear?

At K-9 Mart.

Why did the monkey fall out of the tree?

He was trying to leaf.

What do you get when you cross a cat with a vacuum cleaner?

I don't know, but it sure drinks a lot of milk!

How do bears walk around?

With bear feet.

What do you get from a pampered cow?

Spoiled milk.

7

Two cows are standing in a wide-open field in Great Britain. One cow says to the other cow: "Hey, are you worried about that mad cow disease?" The second cow says: "Why would I be worried about mad cow disease? I'm an airplane!" ✩

Where do monkeys pick up wild rumors?

What did the 500-pound canary say as he walked down the street?
"Here, kitty, kitty, kitty."

Why aren't leopards any good at hide-and-seek?
Because they're always spotted.

What do you have to be careful of when it rains cats and dogs?
That you don't step in a poodle.

8

Why should you be careful when playing against a team of big cats?
They might be cheetahs.

While walking along the street, a man saw a sign that said: TALKING DOG FOR SALE, $10. The man couldn't believe his ears when the dog said, "Please buy me. I'm a great dog. I played professional football. I was even nominated most valuable player."

"That dog really *does* talk!" the man gasped. "Why in the world do you want to sell him for only ten dollars?"

"He never played professional football," said the dog's owner, "and I can't stand liars." ✿

Through the apevine.

Saturday Night Live

Saturday *Night Live* began in 1975 as a showcase for talented young comedians. A television producer named Lorne Michaels created the show as a series of comedic skits, called sketches, that would air live. Although each show is loosely scripted and rehearsed, the live taping encourages improvisation and quick thinking among the cast.

A cast of comedians plays different characters in the sketches during the 90-minute show, which airs around 11:30 P.M. on Saturday nights in the Eastern time zone. Each week, a celebrity host—usually a movie or TV star—opens the show with a monologue and appears in a few skits, and a popular music group performs a few songs on the air as well.

SNL, as it is commonly known, has launched the careers of many comedians and comic actors, including several of those featured in this book. Eddie Murphy, Chris Rock, Adam Sandler, Mike Myers, and Janeane Garofalo all performed on *SNL.* Many comics who appear on the show create distinctive characters for their skits—Mike Myers's Wayne Campbell and "Wayne's World," for example. *SNL* writers and actors pay close attention to current events in order to shape the show. For over 25 years, the show has been the place to be for up-and-coming comic talent and a witty look at what's happening in the world.

What do you call a cat who can bowl?

An alley cat.

What do you call a small cat who makes up songs?

An itty bitty ditty kitty.

STAND-UP COMEDY

Imagine how much fun it would be to get paid just for being funny! Well, stand-up comics are professional comedians who do just that. *Stand-up comedy* is exactly what it sounds like—someone stands up in front of other people and tries to make them laugh. Stand-up comedians prepare a series of jokes, skits, and wisecracks for their routines. Often, they will also impersonate, or mimic, famous people. Comedians typically open a show with a *monologue,* a long solo speech. A monologue frequently consists of a string of jokes on one topic with no break in between. Most comedians perform in comedy clubs, which are theaters or nightclubs that hire comedians to entertain people.

10

What do you call a cat who's been thrown in the dryer?

Fluffy.

What do you call a cat who gets thrown in the dryer and is never found again?

Socks.

What did the cat get on the test?

A purr-fect score.

What do cats have that no other animal in the world has?

Kittens.

What do you get when you cross a dog with canvas?

A pup tent.

What do you get when you cross a dog with a fountain pen?

Ink spots.

What do you call a dog who helps you carry hot things?

An oven mutt.

What do you get when you cross Lassie with a petunia?

A collie flower.

One day an out-of-work mime is visiting the zoo, and he figures he'll try to earn some money performing. Unfortunately, as soon as he starts to draw a crowd, a zookeeper grabs him and drags him into his office.

The zookeeper explains to the mime that the zoo's most popular attraction, a gorilla, has died suddenly and the keeper fears that attendance at the zoo will fall off. He offers the mime a job to dress up as the gorilla until they can get another one. The mime accepts.

The next morning the mime puts on a gorilla suit and enters the cage before the crowd arrives. He discovers that it's a great job. He can sleep all he wants, play, and make fun of people, and he draws bigger crowds than he ever did as a mime.

12

However, eventually the crowds tire of him and he gets bored with swinging on tires. He begins to notice that the people are paying more attention to the lion in the cage next to his. Not wanting to lose the attention of his audience, he climbs to the top of his cage, crawls across a divider, and dangles from the top of the lion's cage. Of course, this makes the lion furious, but the crowd loves it. At the end of the day the zookeeper comes and gives the mime a raise for being such a good attraction.

This goes on for some time. The mime keeps taunting the lion, the crowds grow larger, and the mime's salary keeps going up. Then one terrible day while he is dangling over the furious lion, he slips and falls. The mime is terrified. The

SHHH!

BEHIND THE PUNCH LINE:
Improvisations

An *improvisation* is a comedy routine made up on the spot. A group of actors performing "improv," as it is known, often milk the audience for suggestions on the subjects of their routines, then structure the comedy around whatever topic the audience gives them. For example, a member of the group might yell out to the audience, "We need a subject for a talk show!" Someone in the audience might yell back, "Broccoli addiction support group!" The actors will then pretend that they are on *Oprah* discussing their issues with broccoli.

Improvisation gives actors a chance to develop their comedy "chops." They need the fast pace of this technique to keep them on their toes. *Saturday Night Live* is based on improvisation, although the actors have scripted notes and cue cards to help them out at times.

It takes a lot of skill to keep a joke going for a long time and still make it funny. If you lose your audience, the routine loses its energy. Improv is fun for the audience, too, because it makes them feel like they are part of the show.

Most colleges and universities have improv groups for students, and there are a few professional troupes as well. The most famous professional improv troupe is the Groundlings, based in Los Angeles, which has seen more than a few of its actors go on to become big stars.

13

lion gathers himself and prepares to pounce. The mime is so scared that he begins to run round and round the cage with the lion close behind. Finally, the mime starts screaming and yelling "Help me! Help me!" but the lion is quick and pounces. The mime soon finds himself flat on his back, looking up at the angry lion, who growls, "Shut up, you idiot! Do you want to get us both fired?" ✿

There was a man who was born on the fifth day of the fifth month of 1955, whose lucky number was five. On his birthday he went to the racetrack and was astounded to see that in the fifth race (scheduled for five o'clock) a horse called Pentagram was running, with the odds of 55 to 1. Rushing off to the bank, the man was astonished to find he had $5,555.55 in his bank account. He withdrew the whole amount, dashed back to the races and bet all of it on Pentagram to win. Pentagram, obviously, came in fifth. ✩

What do you get when you cross a dog with an omelette?

Pooched eggs.

14

A tribal chieftain was very religious and, upon assuming power, he forbade the killing of all animals. Before long, however, the number of lions and cheetahs was getting out of hand. There were so many of them that they did not have enough to eat and began feeding on humans. The people were terrified and asked their leader to reverse his order, but he refused. The people decided they had no choice but to overthrow the chief. It was the first time in history that a reign was called on account of game. ✩

What do you get when you cross a dog with a sprinter?
The 100-yard Dachshund.

What do you get when you cross a dog with a journalist?
A Rover reporting.

What's better than a talking dog?

A spelling bee.

Why did the Doberman marry the Golden Retriever?
He found her very fetching.

15

Irv decided to call his dog Stripe. His friend Benny looked at him like he was crazy. "Why did you call your dog Stripe?" asked Benny. "He's a Dalmatian with black spots."

"Well, my other pet is named Spot," explained Irv.

"You never told me you had another Dalmatian," said Benny.

"I don't. My other pet is a zebra." ☆

ha-ha!

How do you make a puppy disappear?
Use Spot remover.

Why did the dog cross the road twice?

She was trying to fetch a boomerang.

What do you get when you cross a dog with a soldier?

A pooper trooper.

One day, a busy butcher notices a dog in his shop and shoos it away. Later, he finds the dog has come back, and the butcher sees that the dog has a note in its mouth, which reads: "Can I have 12 sausages and a leg of lamb, please." The butcher looks, and lo and behold, there's a $10 bill in the dog's mouth. So the butcher takes the money, puts the sausages and lamb in a bag, and places the bag in the dog's mouth. The butcher is very impressed, and since it's closing time, he decides to close up shop and see where the dog goes.

The dog walks down the street and comes to a crosswalk. It puts down the bag, jumps up, and presses the crossing button. Then it waits patiently, bag in mouth, for the light to change. The dog walks across the road with the butcher following. The dog then comes to a bus stop, and starts looking at the timetable. The butcher is in awe. The dog checks out the bus times, and sits on one of the seats to wait. Along comes a bus. The dog walks to the front of the bus, looks at the number, and goes back to its seat.

Another bus comes. Again the dog goes and looks at the number. It sees that it's the right bus, and climbs on. The butcher, by now completely flabbergasted, follows the dog onto the bus. The bus travels through town and out to the suburbs. Eventually the dog gets up, moves to the front of the bus, and, standing on its hind legs, rings the bell to stop the bus. The dog gets off, the groceries still in its mouth, and the butcher continues to follow it.

They walk down the road, and the dog approaches a house. It walks up the path, and drops the groceries on the step. Then it walks back down the path, takes a big run, and throws itself —whap!—against the door. It goes back down the path, takes another run, and throws itself— whap!—against the door again! There's no answer at the door, so the dog goes back down the path, jumps up on a narrow wall, and walks along the perimeter of the garden. It gets to a window, and bangs its head against it several times. It walks back, jumps off the wall, and waits at the door. The butcher watches as a big guy opens the door and starts yelling at the dog. The butcher runs up and stops the guy. "What are you doing? This dog is a genius. It could be on TV, for Pete's sake!" "Genius, my eye," the man says. "This is the second time this week he's forgotten his key!" ☆

What do you get if you cross a bear with a skunk?

Winnie the Pee-yew!

BEHIND THE PUNCH LINE:

Shaggy-Dog Jokes

Shaggy-dog jokes are those overly long and annoying stories that make you groan because they're full of meaningless details and absurd characters. In fact, most of the story has very little relation to the punch line. A good storyteller, though, can have people in stitches because the ending is often so stupid and unexpected. Shaggy-dog jokes get their name from an old long and pointless joke which was about a shaggy dog. Today, however, the stories can be about anything, as long as they are ridiculous and lengthy and told in a misleading way.

The Original Shaggy Dog? You Be the Judge

And now, for (a variation on) the original shaggy-dog story:

A man was reading his newspaper one morning at breakfast. Halfway through it he noticed a large ad set in bold type. It promised $5,000 to whoever could find the advertiser's lost "shaggy dog" and return it to him in Timbuktu. The man didn't pay much attention to it. Later that day, however, the man found a dog running down the street that matched the description in the newspaper. It was a large shaggy sheepdog, and it did, in fact, look a bit lost. So the man put it on a leash. He bought a plane ticket for himself and the dog, and flew all the way to Timbuktu. He found the address that had been advertised in the paper and rang the doorbell. An older man answered the door. "Look, sir," the man with the dog said, "I've found your dog."

"My dog was shaggy," the man replied, "but not quite that shaggy."

There was once a perfect little girl. She wore perfect little dresses that fit her perfectly and perfect little shoes to match. She had a perfect smile with perfect teeth. She wore her hair in perfect curls and had perfect bangs. Her room was perfect, too, with a perfect bed and a perfect view. She ate perfect toast and drank perfect orange juice every morning. Her parents' friends were always commenting on how perfect she was. In school, she always got perfect grades and had a perfectly neat desk. She only made friends with the other perfect little kids. One day, she was out walking when she saw the most perfect little puppy on the other side of the street. She thought, I must have that perfect puppy. It will match my perfect dress that fits me perfectly, my perfect little shoes, my perfect smile, my perfect teeth, my perfect curls and my perfect

She was a Perfect target!

bangs. That puppy would be perfect in my perfect room with my perfect bed and my perfect view. It can eat my perfect toast with me in the morning, and drink perfect orange juice. My parents' friends will all say how perfect my puppy is. It can come to my school and sit by my perfect desk, and my perfect friends will pet it. The perfect little girl ran across to get the perfect puppy, and got hit by a car.

What's the moral of the story?

Look both ways before crossing the street. ✩

A dog with a bandaged foot limped into town one day. The sheriff approached the stranger and said: "What brings you to Dawson City?" The dog replied: "I'm looking for the man who shot my paw." ☆

What do you get when you mate a cat with a ball of wool?

Mittens.

What do you get when you put a kitten in a Xerox machine?

A copycat.

What do you get when you put your kitten in the refrigerator?

The coolest cat in town.

20

An out-of-towner drove his car into a ditch in a remote area in the country. Luckily, a local farmer came to help with his big, strong horse named Buddy. He hitched Buddy up to the car and yelled, "Pull, Nellie, pull!" Buddy didn't move. Then the farmer hollered, "Pull, Buster, pull!" Buddy didn't budge. Once more the farmer commanded, "Pull, Coco, pull!" Nothing. Then the farmer casually said, "Pull, Buddy, pull!" and the horse easily dragged the car out of the ditch. The motorist was most grateful and very curious. He asked the farmer why he had called his horse by the wrong name three times. The farmer said, "Oh, Buddy is blind and if he thought he was the only one pulling, he wouldn't even try!" ☆

What do you get when you cross a cat and an oven?

A self-cleaning oven.

What do cats call mice?

Delicious.

What do cats drink on hot summer afternoons?

Mice tea.

Why did the cat family move next door to the mouse family?

So they could have the neighbors for dinner.

Bert has announced that he's given up on trying to teach Kitty to come when he calls. He said he's moved on to something much easier—teaching the dog to climb trees. ✫

21

What do you call a pooch who wakes up too early in the morning?

A groggy doggie.

What do you do with a broken dog?

Get him fixed.

What's fast, furry, and goes "foow, foow?"

A dog chasing a car that's in reverse.

Where can you leave your dog while you shop?

In the barking lot.

Down, Boy, Down!

Why didn't they let the wildcat into school?

They knew he was a cheetah.

What do you get when you cross a leopard with a dishwasher?

Spots on your dishes.

A lion had to appear at the courthouse to prove he had been a good ruler of the animal kingdom. He was nervous about his first day in court, but his friends told him he'd be all right if he just focused on the questions the judge asked and answered them as best he could.

The lion dressed up in his very best suit, and got to court right on time. He smiled at the judge and was very polite. He was a little shocked when the judge asked him "Are you a lion?"

"No, sir," stammered the lion. "I swear, I'm telling the truth!" ☆

Why won't banks allow kangaroos to open accounts?

Their checks always bounce.

A wildcat committed a horrible murder and then left the country. The police came upon the scene of the crime and were stumped. They found the murder weapon, the paw prints, and the victim's body, but were unable to catch the crook. How come?

They couldn't find the missing lynx. ☆

22

What do you call a grizzly bear with no teeth?

A gummy bear.

What do bears wear in their hair?

Bearettes.

What did the mother buffalo say to her son before he left?

Bison.

What did the mother kangaroo say when her baby was kidnapped?

"Somebody help me catch that pickpocket!"

An elephant was drinking out of a river one day when he spotted a turtle asleep on a log. He marched over and kicked it clear across the river. "What did you do that for?" asked a giraffe that happened to be passing by.

"Because I recognized it as the same turtle that took a nip out of my trunk 53 years ago."

"Wow, what a memory!" exclaimed the giraffe.

"Yes," said the elephant. "It's a case of turtle recall." ✿

What is a Californian cow's favorite TV show?
Haywatch.

23

Peter Rabbit was a very bad bunny. He never finished his carrots at dinner. He always hopped fences. And every day he would sneak into a farmer's field and steal a head of lettuce. Every day for three weeks in a row, the farmer would check his garden and find a big hole where a lettuce head used to be.

One night the farmer decided he would catch the culprit, so he hid in some bushes by the garden. At sunrise, the farmer saw Peter sneak into the vegetables and chew off a head of lettuce. He jumped out from his hiding place and ran after Peter Rabbit. They ran through fields and through dales and across miles and miles of meadows. At the end of a long and exhausting chase, the angry farmer cornered Peter in a pumpkin patch with a big, sharp, pointy pitchfork. Why didn't he kill him?

For Pete's sake. ☆

24

Boy: Why didn't you pull a rabbit out of your hat?
Magician: Because I just washed my hare and I can't get it to do anything now!

What do rabbits sing to each other once a year?
"Hoppy Birthday."

How do you catch a rabbit?
Hide behind a tree and make carrot noises.

What do you get when you cross a cow with a tidal wave?
Udder disaster.

What do you call a group of mice in disguise?

A mousequerade party.

How does a mouse feel after it takes a bath?

Squeaky clean.

What's a mouse's least favorite sound?

The hiss of death.

Why wouldn't the girl mouse move in with the boy mouse?

Because his house was such a hole in the wall.

What do you call it when a bull swallows a stick of dynamite?

A-bomb-in-a-bull.

25

A guy opens his front door one morning to find a snail sitting on his doorstep. The guy swings his leg back and kicks the snail all the way down the walkway in front of his house. Two years later, the doorbell rings. When the man answers the door, he looks down and there is the snail, who asks, "What was *that* all about?" ✩

Why did the farmer give the cow a hammer at bedtime?

Because he wanted the cow to hit the hay.

What goes trot-dash-trot-dash-dash?

Horse code.

What kind of horse makes you wake up scared?

A nightmare.

Why do zebras have black and white stripes?

So they can referee football games.

Why don't rabbits have black and white stripes?

Why on earth would a rabbit want to referee a football game?

Why did the chimp sell his banana store?

He was tired of all the monkey business.

Why wouldn't the pet store take back the chimp?

They didn't offer a monkey-back guarantee.

What's the best way to stop a rhinoceros from jumping up and down on the bed?

A camel, a giraffe, a donkey, and a pig all went to an audition at a comedy club. The camel went on first. He did an impersonation of a llama, told ten jokes, and then left the stage. The judges all laughed. Then the giraffe came out. First the giraffe cleared her throat, which took a little while. Then the giraffe did a headstand and told a few tall tales. The judges found her so funny, they asked her to come back the next day. The donkey went on stage next. The donkey had a really zany act, and the judges got a kick out of it. Finally, the pig stood at the microphone. He told a really, really, really, long shaggy-dog story about a circus dog. The joke was so long that it took the pig two hours to tell it. The judges were so upset that they threw the pig out of the club.

Why didn't the judges like the pig?

The pig was a real boar. ☆

What should you do when you're serving a camel tea?

Ask him if he'd like one hump or two.

What do you call a really good camel joke?

A hump-dinger.

Put Krazy Glue on the ceiling.

A woman walks into a bar with a giraffe. The woman goes over to the bar to order a drink while the giraffe lies down. The bartender says to the woman, "Hey, you can't leave that lyin' on the floor!" The woman answers, "It's not a lion." ✩

HAI-BAAA!

What do you get when you cross a sheep with a kung fu master?
Lamb chops.

Why do kings have royal seals?
Because royal walruses eat too much.

What did the sheep say to his fiancée?
"There's something I have to tell you: I love ewes."

What did the fiancée say back?
"Don't worry, I love ewes too."

What do you call a sheep farm with only rams?
Ewes-less.

How do you toast a sheep?
"Here's to ewe."

Where did the sheep go after high school?
Ewe-niversity.

What do you call a lamb who does aerobics?

Sheep shape.

When is a sheep like a dog?

When it has fleece.

What do pigs see when they go to the ballet?

Swine Lake.

Why are pigs always in fashion?

They're sty-lish.

What do you call a go-go dancing pig?

Shakin' bacon.

29

What did the pig say when he fell down the stairs?

"Oh, my achin' bacon."

What happened when the pig couldn't get up from his fall?

He called a ham-bulance.

Where did he go to recover from his fall?

The hog-spital.

Which skunk lives in a church?

Pepe le Pew.

What kind of books do skunks read?

Best-smellers.

SIS-BOOM-BAA-BAA

How do sheep cheer for their favorite football team?

Two little skunks, one named In and one named Out, wanted to go and play. Their parents told them they could, but an hour later, only Out came back.

"Hasn't In come in?" asked Father Skunk.

"Out went out with In but only Out came back in," said Mother Skunk.

"Well, Out," said Father, "you better go out and find In and bring her in."

So Out did. And only a few moments later, he returned with his wayward sister.

"Ah, good," said Mother Skunk, pleased. "How did you find her?"

Out smiled. "Instinct," he said. ✩

What does the cow like to do on her day off?

Go to the moovies.

SLIM: I thought you were going bear hunting!
JIM: I was. But I only made it as far as the highway.
SLIM: What happened?
JIM: Well, I saw a road sign that said BEAR LEFT, so I came home!

CRITTER JITTERS

Creepy, Crawly, Slimy, Slithery Things

A tourist was fishing off the coast of Florida when his boat tipped over. He could swim, but he was afraid of alligators and hung on to the side of the overturned boat. Spotting an old beachcomber standing on the shore, the tourist shouted out, "Are there any 'gators around here?"

"Naw," the man hollered back. "They haven't been around here for years!"

Feeling safe, the tourist started swimming calmly toward the shore. About halfway there, he asked the guy, "How'd you get rid of the 'gators?"

"We didn't do anything," said the beachcomber. "The sharks got 'em." ✩

ha-ha!

"NO GATORS"

What do you call a mouse who hangs out with a bunch of pythons?

Lunch.

HOTEL GUEST: Is this the desk clerk?

CLERK: Yes, it is. This is the third time you've called. What is it?

HOTEL GUEST: This hotel is full of bugs! What a nightmare!

CLERK: What's biting you?

HOTEL GUEST: That's what I'd like to know!

What did the spider bride wear when she got married?

A webbing dress.

What do you get when you cross a flea with a rabbit?

A bugs bunny.

How did the praying mantis get the gossip on the grasshopper?

His phone was bugged.

Why did all the bees in the hive start throwing up?

There was a bug going around.

Did you hear about the caterpillar's stress attack?

JACK: Say, Jill, how did you get a swollen nose?
JILL: I bent down to smell a brose in my garden.
JACK: Not brose, *rose,* Jill. There's no *B* in rose.
JILL: There was in this one!

A snail goes into a car dealership. She asks the salesman if they sell red convertibles. The salesman answers, "Yes. But do you have a proper license, and the money to pay for the car?" The snail replies, "Yes, I've got both. The thing is, I'll only buy the car on one condition—that you have a big *S* painted on the sides of the car." The salesman thinks about that for a moment. It seems odd to him, but it isn't every day that he sells an expensive convertible, so he agrees.

A few weeks later, the car is all ready and the salesman calls the snail to tell her she can come pick it up. The snail is really pleased with her car and thanks the salesman. The salesman is still wondering about the reason for the big *S* on the car and asks, "So why did you want an *S* painted on the sides of the car?" The snail replies, "When I drive by, I want everyone to say, 'Look at that *S* car go!'" ☆

He totally bugged out.

A turtle is mugged by three snails, but when the police ask the turtle to give a description of what happened, all he can say is, "I don't know, officer. It all happened so fast!" ☆

What did the fly say to the flypaper?
"I'm stuck on you."

What do you get when you cross a centipede and a parrot?
A walkie-talkie.

What did the dog do after he swallowed a firefly?
He barked with de-light!

34

What did one flea say to the other flea as they were leaving to go to the movies?
"Shall we walk, or take a dog?"

ZZZZT!

If only you knew the power of the DARKSIDE!

What do you get if you cross a Jedi knight with a toad?
Star Warts.

SPOTLIGHT

Rugrats

Rugrats, which premiered in 1991 on Nickelodeon, is a rare cartoon that appeals to everyone from very young children to adults. *The Rugrats Movie* was released in 1999 and quickly set box-office records. The Rugrats plan a visit to Paris on their next big-screen outing.

Rugrats combines preschool-age characters with a sassy sense of humor that appeals to older kids. The excellent animation and funky background music attract other viewers.

Bold and brave Tommy, his little brother Baby Dil (introduced in the movie), his bossy cousin Angelica (and of course her doll Cynthia!), and scaredy-cat Chuckie are at the center of the large *Rugrats* cast. Though all are under four years of age, they talk as if they were adults—and keep the audience believing that they in fact know more than the grown-ups!

BABY SNAKE: Mom, are we poisonous?
MOM SNAKE: We most certainly are! Why?
BABY SNAKE: I just bit my tongue!

Two ants wandered into a large-screen TV. After crawling around for hours and hours the first ant started to cry. "I think we're lost! We'll never get out!"

"Don't worry," said the second ant. "I brought along a TV guide." ☆

36

What does a reptile wear on its feet?
Snakers.

What goes zzub, zzub, zzub?
A bee flying backwards.

Why did the turtle cross the road?
To get to the Shell station.

What do you call an insect who goes "Buzz-mzz-ummz-mzz"?
A mumble bee.

PRACTICAL JOKE

Want to really gross out your classmates? Tell them you've eaten *dudu.*

After they recover from the shock, tell them it's an African specialty made of fried, salted *bugs:* ants, bees, crickets, and cicadas. Mmm, tasty!

How does a bee get to school?

It takes the buzz.

THE MAKING OF A COMEDIAN

Step 2: Rehearsing

Although many comedy routines sound as though they were made up on the spur of the moment, every good comedian spends a great deal of time rehearsing. Even improv comedians have to practice! Rehearsal helps you make your routine smooth. You need to practice your pacing: when to pause, what to emphasize. You need to set the right tone: cheerful, somber, sarcastic.

Think of yourself as a joke samurai. A samurai is a Japanese warrior whose code of conduct forbids showing any sign of weakness before others. A good joke samurai should never let the audience see his or her weakness. Every professional comedian has spent time practicing the art of joke telling, and has studied his or her punch lines really well. Just remember, if an audience thinks that you don't know what you're doing, they'll be too uncomfortable to laugh even if you've said something hilarious. Ask an adult to explain any of the material in this book that you don't understand before you go out and dazzle your friends.

A man was driving down a lonely country road when it began to snow heavily. His windows fogged up, and his wiper blades were badly worn and soon fell apart. The man couldn't see out of the front of his car anymore and he couldn't continue to drive, so he stopped the car. Then he got out and started to turn over large rocks. Finally, he found two frozen snakes. He straightened them out and stuck them flat onto his blades, and they worked just fine. Haven't you ever heard of "wind-chilled vipers"? ☆

Why doesn't a python use silverware?

Because he has a forked tongue.

38

Once upon a time in a magical land, there lived a snake named Nate. In this land, actually rather close to Nate's house, there was a great road, and next to this road was a lever. The lever was ancient, and the myth around the lever was that if you were to push it, it would trigger the end of the world. One day, Nate was slithering down the road. When he came upon the lever, he began crossing the road so he could get a look at it. At the same moment, a truck came zooming around the corner, and the driver found himself in a dilemma: either hit the snake and run him over, or swerve, hit the lever, and end the world. Needless to say, the driver ran over Nate and went on his merry way. What's the moral of this story? Better Nate than lever. ☆

What does a boa constrictor call his girlfriend?

A millipede ran into a centipede on the street. The millipede said in surprise, "Wow, what are the odds of this?!"

"Oh," answered the centipede, "about 10 to 1." ☆

Why did the praying mantis go to the film?
He heard it was a feeler-good movie.

What did the termite do when she couldn't carry the twig on her own?
She hired an assist-ant.

A frog is walking along one day when he comes across a fairy.

"For forty bucks," the fairy says, "I can turn you into a prince."

"Wow!" exclaims the frog, and gives the fairy fifty dollars.

The fairy changes the frog into a handsome, dashing prince. The former frog is overjoyed.

"It'll be so much easier to get a date for the ball now," he thinks.

So the prince asks the fairy for the ten bucks that was left over so he can rent a really snazzy limo to the next ball. The magic fairy gives him the money and is about to leave when suddenly the prince shrinks down in his boots, turns green, and is once again a frog. Shocked and despairing, the frog stares at the magic fairy. "What happened?" he asks.

"Well," she replies, "You gave me fifty bucks and then asked for your change back." ☆

His Main Squeeze!

What do you get when you cross an iguana with three bullfrogs?

Leaping lizards!

"...THEN I SAID "SO WHAT-I'LL JUST GROW A NEW TAIL!" HA! HEY-I'LL BE HERE ALL WEEK, FOLKS...

GET LOST, LIZARD!

48

What kind of lizard loves to tell jokes?

A sillymander.

Why is it so hard to fool a snake?

Because you can't pull its leg.

Why did the bug family stay home on their last vacation?

The roach motel was full.

Why did the mama ladybug ground her kids?

They were bugging her.

What is a frog's favorite soda?

Croaka-Cola.

Some Boy Scouts from the city were on a camping trip. The mosquitoes were so fierce that the boys had to hide under their blankets to avoid getting bitten. Then one of them saw some lightning bugs and said to his friend, "We might as well give up. They're coming after us with flashlights." ☆

FOWL PLAY

Birds of a Feather Flock Together

What do you get when a canary gets caught in a lawnmower?

Shredded tweet.

Why did the bird make fun of everyone?

It was a mockingbird!

What do you call a bird that's been eaten by a cat?

A swallow.

What do you call the second bird that's been eaten by the same cat?

An after-dinner tweet.

One day a man walked into a bird shop carrying a beak. "I'm looking for a bird to match this beak," he said to the owner.

"No problem," said the owner. "I've got one that'll fit the bill." ☆

Where can you find out more about ducks?

In a duck-tionary.

Why did the teacher send the duck out of the classroom?

He was making wisequacks.

How do baby birds know how to fly?

They just wing it.

Why did the bird sit on the fish?

The fish was a perch.

If a seagull flies over the sea, what flies over the bay?

A bagel.

42

Hey, my allergy to feathers is gone!

What do you get if you cross a duck with an alligator?

A quack-odile.

What do you call a baby bird that takes after its father?

A chirp off the ol' beak.

Why did the duck become a spy?

He was good at quacking codes.

Jim Carrey

Jim Carrey is now the highest-paid comic actor in show business. He started his career at a very young age. With the encouragement of his father, he was performing in comedy clubs in his native Toronto, Ontario, Canada, at age 15.

Later, Carrey was a writer and performer on the Fox network's sketch comedy show *In Living Color* from 1990 to 1994. Carrey's specialty was physical comedy. Double-jointed and blessed with a face that appears to be made from rubber, Carrey's body can pretty much do whatever he wants it to—and the grosser the better. Burps, farts, bathroom jokes—Carrey does it all. As Carrey's popularity has grown, so has the acceptance of his brand of comedy.

In 1994, Carrey starred in *Ace Ventura, Pet Detective*— his breakout hit. He followed that up with *Dumb and Dumber* (a slapstick farce that earned Carrey his first of many MTV Movie Awards and People's Choice Awards), and scored a hat trick with his stellar performance in *The Mask*.

That year cemented Carrey's reputation as a comedian with no fear and no limits. His nutty onscreen antics sold thousands of tickets, and soon he was earning $20 million per film.

Carrey took a more serious turn in *The Truman Show* (1998) as a man literally raised on television before viewers' eyes. *Man in the Moon* (1999) showcased more of Carrey's dramatic talents, but drama didn't seem to be what Carrey's loyal fans wanted—the movie didn't do well in theaters.

Jim Carrey is a comedian in the classic sense of the word—someone who knows how to make people laugh even while being annoying and disgusting.

A lady goes into a pet store one day. "I'm really lonely," she says to the clerk. "I need a pet to keep me company."

"Well," replies the clerk, "how about this nice parrot? He'll talk to you."

"Hey, that's great," says the lady. She buys the parrot and takes him home. The next day the lady comes back to the pet store. "You know, that parrot isn't talking to me yet," she says.

"Hmm, let's see," says the clerk. "I know! You buy this little ladder for his cage. He'll climb the ladder, and then he'll talk." So off she goes with a newly purchased ladder. The next day she comes back again.

"Hey, that parrot still hasn't said a word," she says to the pet store clerk.

He thinks a minute. "How about this little mirror?" he says. "You hang it at the top of the ladder. The parrot will climb the ladder, look in the mirror, and then he'll talk to you."

"Okay," she says, and buys the little mirror and goes home. But the next day that same lady is back in the shop. "Well, I'm getting a bit discouraged," she says. "That parrot *still* won't talk to me."

I need a new mirror— this one is getting blurry...

The clerk scratches his head. "Let me think. Aha! Try this bell. You hang it over the mirror. The parrot will climb the ladder, look in the mirror, ring the bell, and then he will surely talk to you!"

"All right, I'll give it a try," says the lady. And she buys the bell and takes it home. The next day the same lady comes back to the pet shop, and she is very distressed.

"What's wrong?" asks the clerk.

"My parrot . . . well, he died," she answers quietly.

"Oh my gosh! I'm so sorry for your loss!" exclaims the clerk. "But I have to ask you, did the parrot ever say anything to you?"

"Oh yes, he said one thing, right before he died," she replies.

"Well, what did he say?" asks the clerk.

The lady replies, "He said, 'DOESN'T THAT STORE CARRY ANY FOOD?'" ☆

ha-ha!

What sound does a chicken crossed with a cow make?
Cock-a-doodle-moo.

Why did the rooster cross the road?
To show he wasn't a chicken.

A duck walks into a drugstore and asks for a tube of lipstick. The cashier says, "That'll be $1.49," and the duck replies, "Just put it on my bill." ☆

45

What should you do when someone throws a goose at you?

Duck.

What do you say when someone throws a duck at a duck?

"Duck, duck!"

What do you say when someone throws a goose at a duck?

"Duck, duck, goose!"

46

It's in the hat, smart guy!

A magician has been working on a cruise ship doing the same act for many years. The audiences like him, and they change often enough that he doesn't have to worry about finding new tricks. But the captain's parrot sits in the back row and watches him night after night, year after year. After a while, the parrot figures out how the tricks work and starts giving the secrets away to the audiences. When the magician makes a bouquet of flowers disappear, for instance, the parrot squawks, "Behind his back! Behind his back!" Well, the magician gets really annoyed at this, but he doesn't know what to do, since the parrot belongs to the captain. One day, the ship springs a leak and sinks. The magician manages to grab hold of a plank of wood and floats on it. The parrot flies over and sits on the other end. They drift and drift for three days without speaking. On the morning of the fourth day, the parrot looks over at the magician and says, "Okay, I give up. Where did you hide the ship?" ✪

BEHIND THE PUNCH LINE:
Slapstick

Slapstick comedy is just the opposite of stand-up comedy. It's comedy where the comedian doesn't stand up, but falls down! The name "slapstick" comes from a kind of wooden stick used by clowns to hit each other on stage. The slapstick was split down the middle and designed to make a very loud, funny, slapping noise without inflicting any damage on the recipient of the blow. During the nineteenth century, a little bit of gunpowder was plugged into the crack in the stick to make the slaps even more explosive.

Slapstick comedy is very physical and it's hard work. Whether he's getting slapped in the face, poked in the eye, or hit with a pie, the slapstick comic is the victim—or perpetrator—of an endless series of gags and practical jokes. Jim Carrey is an excellent example of a slapstick comedian. He makes faces, contorts his body, and does stunts and pratfalls (a staged fall—carefully done so the comedian doesn't get hurt), all in the name of comedy.

47

Why wouldn't anybody go to the duck doctor?

They all knew he was a quack.

Why can't you play hide-and-seek with poultry in a Chinese restaurant?

Because of the Peking duck.

Why did the other chicken cross the road?

To avoid the flying geese.

Why didn't the hen cross the road?

Because she was too chicken.

Why did the baby cross the road?

She was stapled to the chicken.

Why did the chicken cross the road?

To get the Chinese newspaper.
Get it?
Neither do I. I get USA Today.

Why did the rooster cross the road?

He wanted something to crow about.

48

THE WORLD'S OLDEST JOKE:

Why did the chicken cross the road?

To get to the other side.

Why did the turkey cross the road?

Why did the daredevil cross the road?

He wanted to play chicken.

Why did Hammy Hamster cross the road?

His car was parked on the other side.

David got a parrot for his birthday. This parrot was fully grown, with a bad attitude and an even worse vocabulary. Every other word was naughty or rude. David tried very hard to change the bird's manners. David would always say polite words, play soft music, anything he could think of to try to set a good example, but nothing worked. David was getting really frustrated. He yelled at the bird, and the bird got worse. He shook the bird, and the bird got angrier and more rude. One day, David felt so desperate that he put the parrot in the freezer. For a few moments he heard the bird squawking, kicking, and screaming, then suddenly everything was quiet. David was frightened that he might have hurt the bird and quickly opened the freezer door. The parrot calmly stepped out on to David's arm and said: "I'm sorry that I might have offended you with my language and actions and I ask for your forgiveness. I will try to correct my behavior." David was amazed at the great change in the bird and was about to ask what had caused it when the parrot continued: "May I ask what the chicken did?" ✩

Why did the muddy chicken cross the road and then cross back?

He was a dirty double-crosser.

Why did the chicken bounce across the road?

It was a rubber chicken.

Why did Colonel Sanders cross the road?

He heard there was a chicken on the other side.

The chicken was on strike.

✓ **Why did Colonel Sanders cross the road again?**

He was being chased by a million finger-lickin' chickens.

What do you call it when a chicken stumbles as it crosses the street?

A road trip.

What do you get when you cross a chicken with chewing gum?

Chicklets.

50

What do you get when you cross a hen with a banjo?

A chicken that plays a tune when you pluck it.

Why was the chicken team so bad at baseball?

They kept hitting fowl balls.

What do chickens do when they're in love?

They give each other pecks.

What happens to hens who don't produce enough eggs?

They get laid off.

ROOSTER: Wow, did you hear the voice on that little chick?
HEN: That's what you call beginner's cluck.

Why was the little boy afraid of the turkey?

He heard it was a gobblin'.

Why didn't the turkey finish his dinner?

He was already stuffed.

What do you get when you put a bird in the freezer?

A brrrd.

What do you get when you cross a thousand screech owls with a thousand roosters?

A big headache first thing in the morning.

What did the owl do when his owner abandoned him?

Nothing. He didn't give a hoot.

51

What's the name of the best-selling biography of 400 famous owls?

Who's Who.

Why did Mrs. Crow have such a huge phone bill?

She made too many long-distance caws.

Two men walked into a bird shop looking for their lost parrot. The owner showed them three birds.

"Polly want a cracker," the first parrot said.

"You can buy everything but the kitchen sink," the next one remarked.

"Take me to the ball game!" the last one squawked.

The two men took a moment to consider and then chose the first bird. How did they know which was theirs?

They could tell he was the real macaw. ☆

52

Why wouldn't the canary pay for his date's dinner?

He was too cheep.

Why did the bird fall out of the tree?

It was dead, silly.

Sounds Fishy to Me

It'll Hook You Right Away

What do you call a fish with no eye?

What kind of hair does the ocean have?

Wavy.

What kind of waves are impossible to swim in?

Microwaves.

What did the ocean say to the shore?

Glad to sea you!

A Fsh.

Why do oceans never go out of style?

They're always current.

BILL: I'm taking lessons in fishing and playing Go Fish.

BOB: That's a weird combination.

BILL: Not really. Now I'm a reeler and a dealer.

When is fishing not a good way to relax?

When you're the worm.

What kind of fish goes with peanut butter?

Jelly fish!

What day does a fish hate the most?

Fryday!

54

Two goldfish are in a tank. One says to the other, "Do you know how to drive this thing?"

Turn Left at the bubbling treasure chest, soldier!

What do sharks eat for dinner?

Fish and ships.

What do you call a shark fin floating in your soup?

A dorsal morsel.

What do you get when you mix a fish and an elephant?

Swimming trunks.

Where is the ocean deepest?

At the bottom!

BEHIND THE PUNCH LINE:
Sitcoms

A situation comedy, or *sitcom* for short, is a television show format that features a humorous conflict and resolution in each episode. We watch sitcoms because the characters get themselves tangled up in the most ridiculous situations! Often, it's extra funny because the audience knows exactly what's going on, while the character involved is clueless.

TV producers who create sitcoms hire comedy writers to think up zany scenarios and write funny lines for the show's script. Since there are a variety of characters to work with, these writers have a flexibility that stand-up comedians don't have: they can make the characters trade lines back and forth, blurting out unexpected quips or funny comebacks with very funny results.

Classic sitcoms include *I Love Lucy, The Cosby Show, Seinfeld,* and others.

55

What do sharks eat at barbecues?

Clamburgers.

What is a shark's favorite game?

Swallow the leader.

What do you call a fish's date?

His gill-friend.

What did the ocean say to the shore?

Nothing, it just waved.

What do you call a fish who can do magic?

Marlin the Magnificent.

56

Many years ago, a fisherman's wife blessed her husband with twin sons. The parents loved their children very much, but couldn't think of what to name them. Finally, after a few days, the fisherman said, "Let's not decide on names right now. If we wait a little while, the names will simply come to us."

After several weeks had passed, the fisherman and his wife noticed something peculiar. When left alone, one of the boys would always turn toward the sea, while the other boy would face inland. It didn't matter which way the parents positioned the children, the same child always faced the same direction. "Let's call the boys Toward and Away," suggested the fisherman.

His wife agreed, and from that point on, the boys were known simply as Toward and Away.

The years passed and the lads grew tall and strong. The day came when the aging fisherman said to his sons, "Boys, it is time that you learn how to make a living from the sea." The three of them filled their ship with supplies, said their good-byes, and set sail for a three-month voyage. The three months passed quickly for the fisherman's wife, yet the ship had not returned. Another three months passed, and still no ship. Three whole years passed before the grieving woman saw a lone man walking toward her house. She recognized him as her husband. "My goodness! What has happened to my darling boys?" she cried. The ragged fisherman began to tell his story: "We were just barely one whole day out to sea when Toward hooked into a great fish. Toward fought long and hard, but the fish was more than his equal. For a whole week they wrestled upon the waves without either of them letting up. Yet eventually the great fish started to win the battle, and Toward was pulled over the side of our ship. He was swallowed whole, and we never saw either of them again."

"Oh dear, that must have been terrible! What a huge fish that must have been!" said the fisherman's wife.

"Yes, it was, but you should have seen the one that got Away!" ☆

57

A fish needed surgery, but didn't know if he'd be able to pay for it. He met with the doctor to talk about how much it would cost. "Don't worry at all," said the doctor. "I'll give you a discount on the price. I admire and respect your cousin, so I am honored to be taking care of his family. He is, beyond any doubt, an excellent sturgeon." ✩

Why did the fish stop smoking cigarettes?

She didn't want to get hooked.

A fisherman returned to shore with a giant marlin that was bigger and heavier than he was. On the way to the cleaning shed, he ran into a second fisherman who had a string with a dozen baby minnows attached to it. The second fisherman looked at the marlin, turned to the first fisherman and said, "Only caught one, eh?" ✩

I Love Lucy and Lucille Ball

I *Love Lucy* is considered the first-ever sitcom. The show, which first aired in 1951, starred a red-headed comedienne named Lucille Ball as Lucy Ricardo, a housewife whose crazy antics drove her husband, Ricky, nuts. Ball was married to Cuban musician and actor Desi Arnaz, who played her husband on the show. (It must have been a difficult transition!) Ball's slapstick acting style, combined with some very funny writing, made *I Love Lucy* a landmark of American television. One episode of *I Love Lucy* featured Lucy and her friend Ethel working in a candy factory. They were supposed to fill boxes with candy as it came off a conveyor belt. When the machine broke and began spewing candy everywhere, Lucy had to stuff the candies down her dress. Wacky, yes—but what else was she supposed to do? *I Love Lucy* was one of the first television programs to focus on relationships—between husbands and wives, between neighbors, between friends. Nearly every sitcom on TV today can trace its development back to *I Love Lucy.*

DANGER
BE CAREFUL
WHEN BELT
IS IN MOTION.

PRACTICAL JOKES

Slumber-party jokes to try:

1. Wait until some unlucky person has the nerve to fall asleep first. Take a glass of warm water and carefully place his or her hand into the water. Wait.

Warning: this joke is supposed to make the victim wet the bed. Try this only if you are prepared to tackle the cleanup.

2. If a friend is sleeping in a four-poster bed, wait until he or she is asleep. Take a ball of yarn and wrap it around and around the bedposts, until your victim appears to be sleeping in a spider web. The reaction when the person wakes up and can't get out of bed: priceless.

3. If you have a friend who gets up to pee in the middle of the night, stretch Saran Wrap tightly over the toilet bowl. Make sure there aren't any wrinkles or holes. Put the seat down over the edges of the Saran Wrap. Wait.

4. Pour cold water over the shower curtain rod on someone using the shower. Run away fast.

5. Put some fake plastic vomit in the sink. When this stuff is wet, it looks amazingly real. Expect lots of screaming.

CLASSY JOKES
Classroom Distractions

TEACHER: James, do you use bad words?

JAMES: No, sir.

TEACHER: Do you disobey your parents?

JAMES: No, sir.

TEACHER: Come now, you must do something wrong every once in a while!

JAMES: I tell lies.

TEACHER: Mrs. Jones, I asked you to come in to discuss Johnny's appearance.

MRS. JONES: Why? What's wrong with his appearance?

TEACHER: He hasn't made one in this classroom since September.

PRACTICAL JOKES

Freak out your parents!

Tape the sprayer on your kitchen sink into the "on" position late at night. The first person to turn on the water in the morning will get soaked. (Just make sure it's not you!!!)

Scare the living daylights out of your little brother!

Take a picture of the creepiest, scariest, grossest monster you can find and hide it somewhere in your house. Lead your younger sibling to the hiding place, swear him to secrecy, then reveal the photo and say it's a photo of him when he was born.

Work your big sister into a lather!

Tell her that one of her friends called (for this to work, be specific——use the real name of someone your sibling is close to) and said one of the coolest kids at school is having a party tonight, but you can't remember all the details. Then run and hide for the rest of the day.

62

TEACHER: Amy, I've had to send you to the principal's office every day this week. What do you have to say for yourself?
AMY: I'm glad it's Friday!

PRINCIPAL: Nicole, did you really call your teacher a meanie?
NICOLE: Yes, I did.
PRINCIPAL: And is it true you called her a wicked old witch?
NICOLE: Yes, it is.
PRINCIPAL: And did you also call her a tomato-nosed beanbag?
NICOLE: No, but I'll remember that for next time!

TEACHER: Sam, if I put a dozen marbles in my right pocket, fifteen marbles in my left pocket, and thirty-one marbles in my back pocket, what would I have?
SAM: Heavy pants!

STUDENT: Teacher, will you pass the nuts?
TEACHER: No, I think I'll flunk them.

Why do magicians do so well in school?

They're good at trick questions.

Why did the janitor quit his job?

He wanted to make a clean sweep.

63

A little girl was counting to ten for her math teacher.

"One, two, three, four, five," she said. "Six, seven, eight, ten!"

"Didn't you forget something?" prompted the teacher. "What happened to nine?"

"No," replied the girl. "Seven eight nine."

How much fun can you have doing arithmetic?

Sum fun!

BOY: Isn't our principal stupid?
GIRL: Hey, do you know who I am?
BOY: No, why should I?
GIRL: I'm the principal's daughter.
BOY: Do you know who I am?
GIRL: No.
BOY: Thank goodness!

One by one, a class of fifth-graders were called on to make sentences with words chosen by their teacher. Nick didn't often participate in class, so his teacher was glad when she saw him raise his hand to give it a try.

"Nick," said the teacher, "make a sentence with the words 'defeat,' 'defense,' 'deduct,' and 'detail.'"

Nick thought for a few minutes and smiled. He shouted, "Defeat of deduct went over defense before detail!"

Rosie O'Donnell

Before Rosie O'Donnell got her own talk show, she did stand-up comedy. She performed in small clubs for years before making her TV debut on *Star Search*. Now that she is on TV daily with *The Rosie O'Donnell Show*, she still aims to capture the cozy feeling of a comedy club despite having a viewing audience of millions. To do this, she focuses her performance on the few hundred people who come to watch the show's taping in her New York studio. It seems to work—in just a few years her show was watched by more people than any other daytime talk show!

O'Donnell gives her autograph to kids only. She says that she has an easier time connecting with kids than with adults. As she has said, "In many ways, I still feel like I'm ten. For a long time, I'd go to friends' parties and sit at the kids' table."

She is involved in several children's charities, and raises tons of money for kids through various programs. She promotes kid-friendly Broadway theater, like *The Lion King*, on her show. A few years ago, she produced and starred in a film version of *Harriet the Spy*, which she said was one of her favorite books as a kid.

Rosie O'Donnell is an excellent example of someone who knows her audience well and tailors her performances for them.

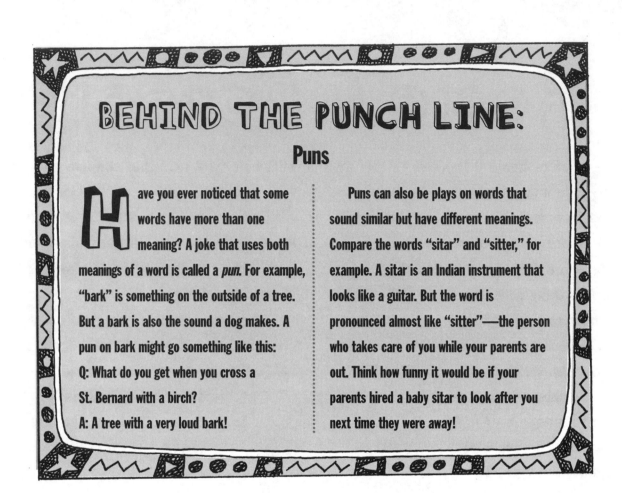

BEHIND THE PUNCH LINE:
Puns

Have you ever noticed that some words have more than one meaning? A joke that uses both meanings of a word is called a *pun*. For example, "bark" is something on the outside of a tree. But a bark is also the sound a dog makes. A pun on bark might go something like this:

Q: What do you get when you cross a St. Bernard with a birch?

A: A tree with a very loud bark!

Puns can also be plays on words that sound similar but have different meanings. Compare the words "sitar" and "sitter," for example. A sitar is an Indian instrument that looks like a guitar. But the word is pronounced almost like "sitter"—the person who takes care of you while your parents are out. Think how funny it would be if your parents hired a baby sitar to look after you next time they were away!

CHEMISTRY TEACHER: What is the formula for water?
STUDENT: H-I-J-K-L-M-N-O.
CHEMISTRY TEACHER: Why would you give a silly answer like that?
STUDENT: You said it was H to O!

TEACHER: Jason, go to the map and find North America.
JASON: Here it is!
TEACHER: Correct. Now, class, who discovered North America?
CLASS (in unison): Jason!

SUBSTITUTE TEACHER: Are you chewing gum, young lady?
MARY: No, I'm Mary Jones.

SAM: Would you punish me for something I didn't do?
TEACHER: No, of course not.
SAM: Good, because I didn't do my homework.

Mark had always been really skinny. One day his uncle said to him, "Mark, you should really eat more. Before you know it, your teacher will mark you absent for standing sideways." ☆

On the first day of school, the kindergarten teacher said to her class, "If anyone has to go to the bathroom, please hold up two fingers."

A little voice from the back row asked, "How will that help?" ☆

67

Why was the library so tall?
Because it had so many stories!

Why was the teacher cross-eyed?
Because he couldn't control his pupils!

Why did the teacher wear sunglasses?
Because the students were so bright!

A teacher asks his class: "If I had 12 apples in my right hand, and 10 apples in my left hand, what would I have?" A voice from the back of the class says: "Really big hands, sir." ☆

Why was the math book sad?

It had too many problems.

James was really excited when he came home from school. His mother asked him for the good news and he said, "I got a hundred in school today! In *two* subjects!"

James's mother was overjoyed. She said, "My goodness, how did you do that?"

James said, "I got a fifty in Math and a fifty in Science." ☆

What's the difference between teachers and trains?

Trains say "Choo Choo!" and teachers say "Spit that gum out!"

68

AH-HAA!

SPLORT!

Why was the student jealous of the Mongolians?

Because they had a ruler with an iron hand and she only had a ruler with a wooden foot.

What's the capital of Arkansas?

A.

Why can you always tell what Dick and Jane are going to do next?

They're easy to read.

69

On the first day of class, the teacher asked any troublemakers to stand up. After a few moments of silence, a shy little girl stood up. "Are you a troublemaker?" the teacher asked.

"No," replied the girl, "I just hate to see you standing there all by yourself." ☆

When do you use both a desk and a table at school?

When you're doing multiplication.

Why aren't babies allowed to take tests?

Because they all have crib sheets.

A frog expert from the aquarium gave a talk to a third-grade class. "It's easy to tell the male frogs from the female frogs," he said. "When you feed them, the male frogs will only eat female flies, and the female frogs will only eat male flies."

"But how do you know which flies are male and which are female?" asked a boy sitting at the back of the class.

"How am I supposed to know?" replied the man. "I'm a *frog* expert." ✫

JANE (ON THE PHONE): I'm afraid my daughter can't go to school today.
PRINCIPAL: Oh, that's too bad. And to whom am I talking?
JANE: This is my mother speaking.

A speaker was booked to address an audience at a university. About two hours before she was supposed to speak, however, a couple of student jokers loaded a truck with all of the folding chairs in the auditorium and drove off. No one knew about this until the audience began to arrive for the lecture. It was too late to do anything about it, and the audience had to stand throughout her talk. That evening she wrote a letter to her mother: "It was a tremendous success. Hours before I got there, every seat in the house was taken, and I was given a standing ovation throughout my speech." ✫

"If you had one dollar and you asked your father for another, how many would you have?" the teacher asked the little boy.

"One dollar," replied the boy.

"You don't know your arithmetic," said the teacher.

"No," replied the boy. "You don't know my father." ✰

How do you fire a math teacher?

Tell her she's history.

A child comes home from her first day at school. Her father asks, "Well, what did you learn today?"

The daughter replies, "Not enough. They want me to come back tomorrow." ✰

Did you hear about the delivery van loaded with thesauruses that crashed into a taxi?

Witnesses were astounded, shocked, taken aback, surprised, startled, dumbfounded, thunderstruck, caught unawares . . .

Sheila was called into her teacher's office for a talk.

"I'm sorry," said the teacher, "but I found out you cheated on your test, so I'm changing your A to an F. Do you have anything to say?"

"Yes," said Sheila. "That's pretty degrading." ✰

71

Why did the teacher put rubber bands on her students' heads?

So they could make snap decisions.

Why did the 25-watt bulb flunk out of school?

He wasn't very bright.

What did the weatherman say about his meteorology test?

"It was a breeze with only a few foggy patches."

TEACHER: Class, someone has stolen my purse out of my desk. It had $100 in it. I know you're all basically good kids, so I'm willing to offer a reward of $10 to whoever returns it.
VOICE AT THE BACK OF THE ROOM: I'm offering $20!

Why are some school classes not very interesting?

Because they were developed by the BORED of Education.

Why do spiders do so well in computer class?

They love the Web.

72

The teacher came outside and found one of her students sitting on the ground with his hands in a giant mud puddle. "What are you doing?" asked the teacher.

The little boy looked up and said, "They say it rained an inch and a quarter last night, and I sure could use the twenty-five cents!" ✩

What kind of school does Sherlock Holmes attend?

Elementary, my dear Watson.

One September, a third-grade class came into their homeroom to discover their new teacher was a stallion. He was a big stallion, but he had a high-pitched little voice, and the class thought this was hilarious. They laughed every time he opened his mouth and he spent his whole day yelling and screaming for order. Finally, one day, the stallion lost his voice, and he brought a pony into the class to help him out. The pony was small, but he had a voice like a foghorn and he bellowed, "YOU KIDS PAY ATTENTION OR ELSE!" The kids quieted down and paid attention, which only goes to show you: To get things done you have to shout until you get a little horse. ✩

Why do ghosts make great cheerleaders?

They have lots of spirit.

Why was the cannibal suspended?

He tried to butter up his teacher.

What do you call a boy who can subtract, multiply, and divide, but can't add?

A total failure.

73

TEACHER: Who wrote *Huckleberry Finn*?
STUDENT: Gee, I didn't know they had post offices back then. . . . But if I had to guess, I'd say it was Tom and some of his other close friends.

J ordan was playing in the schoolyard when he fell down and broke his right arm. Gail came running up to him with a big smile on her face. "Wow, Jordan, you're so lucky. Now you don't have to take any exams."

"Actually, I'm really unlucky," replied Jordan.

"What makes you say that?" asked Gail.

"I'm left-handed," Jordan moaned. "I meant to fall on my other arm." ☆

74

Knock, knock.
Who's there?
Locker.
Locker who?
Locker out, but let me in!

Why did the student take her math homework to gym class?
She wanted to work out her problems.

Where do you find Canada?
On a map.

CARSON: The dog ate my homework.
TEACHER: Carson, you don't have a dog.
CARSON: It was a stray.

PEW!

The Math was OK, but the Social Studies gave me gas...

Is there a silent _C_ in Connecticut?

No, but there's a noisy ocean offshore.

TEACHER: Bobby, what happened in the year 1492?
BOBBY: I don't know. I wasn't alive back then.
TEACHER: That's enough of that, Bobby. Now, I'll give you a hint. Do _Niña, Pinta,_ and _Santa Maria_ sound familiar?
BOBBY: Not to me. I don't know a lot about salsa music.

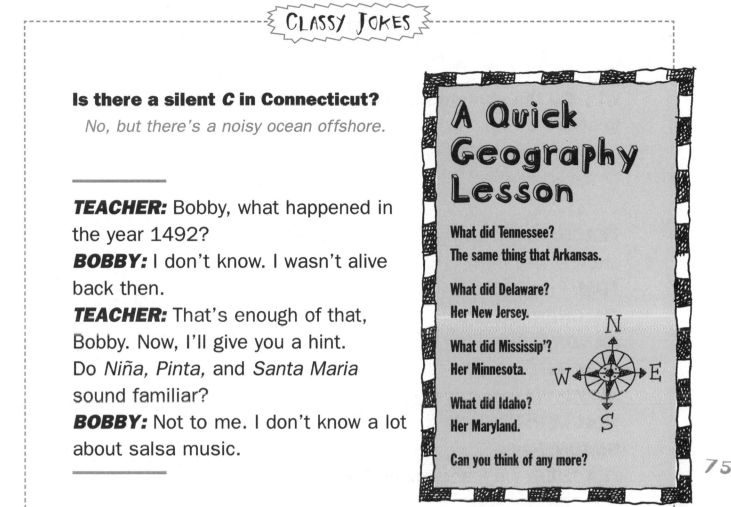

A Quick Geography Lesson

What did Tennessee?
The same thing that Arkansas.

What did Delaware?
Her New Jersey.

What did Mississip'?
Her Minnesota.

What did Idaho?
Her Maryland.

Can you think of any more?

75

Why did the student think his teacher was color-blind?

Because every time she caught him cheating, she said she was seeing red.

GEOGRAPHY TEACHER: What state would you find Lincoln in?
STUDENT: A state of extreme boredom, if he was in this class.

During which school period do cars get put together?

Assembly.

Why did the student put on eyeliner and mascara in school?

Because the teacher said she was giving the class a make-up exam.

TEACHER: I'm giving a quiz today, but first I'll take attendance. Tom?
TOM: Present.
TEACHER: Sandra?
SANDRA: Present.
TEACHER: Aviva?
AVIVA: Present.
TEACHER: Simon?
SIMON: Pass.
TEACHER: We'll see about that.

76

Do old history teachers ever marry?

No, they just get dated.

What's a history teacher's favorite quiz show?

The Dating Game.

...and Bachelor #3 is 435 Years old...

BAD APPLES
And PCs Too!

What did the motherboard say to the new software?

"I'll show you who's DOS!"

They say that Isaac Newton discovered the law of gravity when an apple fell on his head.

Was it a laptop or a desktop model?

Why did the computer keep printing "Like, totally awesome" on every page?

Because it was assembled by a Silicon Valley girl.

What's the longest word in the world?

"Smiles," because it's a mile from one S to the other.

OK-You win! The Apple has a much better operating system than Windows!

Thanks for eating at Mel's Microchips—do you want extra Silicon with that?

No, thanks—it's incompatible with my microprocessors.

What do they serve at the cyber café?

Silicon chips with dip.

Why was the computer geek disappointed by the zoo?

He couldn't find any RAM.

What does a floppy disk do when it needs a break?

Goes for a C: drive.

Why was Susan's dad kicking the computer?

Because he was trying to boot it up.

A Martian bachelor is sad and lonely, so he decides that he needs to find himself someone to share his life with, but he feels that there is no one who's right for him on his home planet. His most recent girlfriend is absolutely beautiful, but really not very smart at all. And then there's the one before her, who is really intelligent but honestly not very attractive. He just can't seem to get it right. So he decides to take a long trip and check out what's available on Earth. He has never been to Earth before and he feels a little embarrassed when he gets lost and has to go into an office supplies store for directions. There she is, the reason he is here, and she is sitting right on the display case in front. He forgets about everything when he sees her. "My goodness," he sighs to himself. "Not only is she beautiful, but she's got brains." Just then a salesperson approaches.

"Sir?" he says. "Can I tell you more about this computer?" ☆

Eddie Murphy

Eddie Murphy's comic career has spanned four decades. This star of recent hit films like *The Nutty Professor* and *Dr. Doolittle* began performing in the 1970s at comedy clubs in Long Island, New York. In 1980, Murphy began a four-year run on *Saturday Night Live.* He was the youngest cast member ever when he started at age 16. In 1983, he recorded a comedy album, *Eddie Murphy: Comedian,* that won him a Grammy Award.

Murphy's films during this phase of his career showcased him in a mixture of action and comedy: *48 HRS.* (1982) and *Beverly Hills Cop* (1984) were two early hits that both led to sequels. A comic role in *Coming to America* (1988) put

his funny bone back in joint.

Murphy considers his family his most important asset, stating to the *New York Daily News* in 1994, "So what if my career dies? If it ends, I'll just stay home and chill."

But Murphy's career shows no signs of ending, and in fact the comedian seems to have had a rebirth lately. In the last ten years, Murphy has looked for more kid-oriented film roles. Both *The Nutty Professor* (1998)—based on an old Jerry Lewis movie—and *Dr. Doolittle* (1988)—adapted from a popular children's book—fit the bill nicely.

Murphy is often cited as a role model by other comedians like Chris Rock. He has shown that flexibility and a wide range can extend and expand an already strong career.

How do you keep a computer geek busy all day?

Put him in a round room and tell him to sit in the corner!

Why did the mother always put on a helmet before she used the computer?

Because she was afraid it would crash!

How do you know when your computer has the Disney virus?

Everything in the computer goes Goofy.

What do pigs put in their hard drives?

Sloppy disks.

How did Max's CD-ROM drive get all wet?

His mom thought it was a coffee-cup holder.

A computer rolled into a bakery and went up to the counter. There were doughnuts and muffins and pastries, but the computer pointed at a plate of cookies. "Hello," it said in an electronic voice.

Astonished, the counter person replied, "Wow, we don't get too many computers in this store. Do you want some of these cookies?"

"Well," said the computer, "I might. Could you tell me how many bites are in each one?"

"I'm sorry," said the counter person. "There aren't any bytes in these cookies, just chips."

What do you call Rollerbladers who chat on the computer?

Online skaters.

Why was the computer so tired when it got home from the office?

Because it had a hard drive.

What's the fastest way to crash a computer?

Let an adult use it.

How can you tell when an adult's been using the computer?

There's correction fluid all over the screen.

Why were there jumper cables hooked up to Betty's computer?

She asked her dad to restart it.

81

How can you tell a good computer programmer from a bad computer programmer?

The good one always comes through when the chips are down.

Who is the best-paid employee at Microsoft?

The Windows washer.

What do you get when you cross Dracula with Microsoft Word?

A word count.

THE MAKING OF A COMEDIAN

Step 3: Uniquely You

Jokes are often based on the most humdrum items and everyday occurrences. Who would have thought a banana was funny until someone invented the slippery peel stunt or stuck one in his ear for the first time? Old-time comedian Charlie Chaplin could make anything hilarious—even a department store escalator. He had a genius for making the average person in the average situation look hysterically funny. As he said, "There is no mystery connected with 'making people laugh.' All I have ever done is to keep my eyes open and brain alert for any facts or incidents that I could use."

So look around you and think about the silly possibilities in life.

82

What did the computer keyboard say to the typist?

"You're really pushing my buttons!"

Why did the woman take her computer to a clinic?

It had a virus.

What do you get when you cross a computer with a toad?

A wart processor.

How was the computer convention?

Crowded. You couldn't get a nerd in edgewise.

Did you hear about the computer with the corrupt hard drive?

Its backup was worse than its byte.

Why didn't the computer go to the prom?

She didn't have a data.

What do you call a computer that only types in uppercase?

Shifty.

Why did the IBM and the Apple computers get a divorce?

They weren't compatible.

How are computers like spies?

They both work in code.

Who does a baby computer cry for when she's upset?

Her motherboard.

Where are delinquent disk drives sent?

To boot camp.

How did the computer feel after its memory had been upgraded?
Chipper.

How did the computers buy a new car?
They all chipped in.

What do you get when you cross a bunny rabbit with the World Wide Web?
A hare Net.

What kind of cola do keyboards like?
Tab.

84

Why did the geek attach his computer to a fishing rod?
Someone told him to hook it up.

How do you keep a nerd in suspense?
I'll tell you later!

Why don't computers eat anything?
They don't like what's on their menus.

How are computers like school hallways?
They both have monitors.

Why did the disk drive become a professional goalie?

It kept making great saves.

Why did the microprocessor always write form letters?

It was an impersonal computer.

How do you find a spider on the Internet?

Check out his Web site.

Why shouldn't you take your computer into rush-hour traffic?

Because it might crash.

How can you tell when a fairy has been using your computer?

Pixel dust.

85

PRACTICAL JOKE

Try these greetings out next time you answer the phone:

"[Your name]'s Pizza! I'm the guy if you want pie!"

"Pet's Vets! There's no business like monkey business!"

"Hello, Disco Cat, the place for glitter and litter!"

"Wine Cellar! We love to complain!"

(in a whisper) "Institute for Overly Sensitive Eardrums"

The queen was having problems retrieving a document from her computer. She called all her ministers into the throne room and asked them what she should do. They went away and debated for hours and hours. Finally, the ministers came up with a solution and dispatched messengers to all four points of the kingdom. These gathered every citizen they could find and brought them all to the castle. The proud ministers made all the women, men, children, and babes in arms stand in a long line and presented them to the queen. "What is the meaning of this?" the irate monarch demanded. "Why," her chief minister responded, "we thought you were looking for a single file!" ✬

Why did the geek turn on his computer on a hot day?
He wanted to open the Windows.

Why did the computer geek take up photography?
He wanted his own dork room.

Why couldn't the geek type on his computer?
He lost his keys.

Why did the boy give his teacher a PC?
The store was out of Apples.

What part of the keyboard do astronauts like best?
The space bar.

86

'SNOT FUNNY
Ew, Gross!

What's the magic word for getting rid of scabs?
Scabracadabra!

Does it work?
Scabsolutely!

What do you call a woman with whiskers who visits you in the middle of the night and grants you three wishes?
Your hairy godmother.

What's black and white and red all over?
A newspaper.

What else is black and white and red all over?
A zebra with a sunburn.

What were the little snots afraid of when they went to bed?
The booger man.

A man heard his friend was in the hospital but didn't know what had happened to him, or even which room to visit. So he went to the hospital and politely waited at the desk. When the nurse looked up, he gave his friend's name and asked for the room number. "Room 105, 106, 107, and 108," she replied, and went back to her paperwork.

"I don't understand," the man stammered. "Which one is it?"

"All of them," the nurse said. "He got run over by a steamroller." ✪

What's black and white and green and black and white?

Two zebras fighting over a pickle.

O ne day a lady walked into the doctor's office. She said, "Doctor, I have a farting problem. I fart all the time. They don't smell, and they're silent. They don't even bother me! In fact, I have farted 20 times since I entered the room, and you didn't even know! Do you have a diagnosis?"

The doctor gave the lady some pills and sent her on her way. The lady came back to the doctor's office a week later and said, "Doctor! What pills did you give me? Now, when I fart, they stink!"

The doctor replied, "Great, now that we've got your sinuses cleared up, let's work on your hearing." ✪

Say "AHH..."

AHH-GH!

88

PRACTICAL JOKE

Scare your babysitter:

Find a big Band-Aid. Put ketchup on it, and put it on yourself. Then tell the babysitter you cut yourself with a knife, and were bleeding a lot, but you put a bandage on and are OK now. Then pretend to pass out.

What's black and white and flat?

A panda that's been run over.

What's black and white and can't get through a revolving door?

A zebra with a spear through its head.

What's green and blue and yellow and black?

A burnt peacock.

What's red and green and goes 80 miles an hour?

A frog in a blender.

89

What do you get when you grill a Barbie doll?

A Barbieque.

What do you get if you cross a mouth with a tornado?

A tongue twister.

What is brown and sticky?

A stick.

What goes bonk bonk bonk dunk?

A rubber-nosed clown being dribbled by a professional basketball player.

Darn! There goes my party outfit and all my accessories!

A very pretty lady is sitting in an expensive restaurant one evening. She is waiting for her date, and wants to be sure everything is perfect. She decides to check how her hair looks. As she bends over in her chair to get a mirror from her purse, she accidentally farts quite loudly just when the waiter is walking up. She sits up, horribly embarrassed and red in the face, sure that everyone in the restaurant has heard the fart. She tries to blame it on the waiter, and turns to him and orders, "Stop that!" The waiter looks at her calmly and replies, "Sure, lady. Where was it headed?" ☆

What goes bonk bonk bonk croak?

A rubber-nosed clown who's just been changed into a frog by an evil witch.

A farmer went out to the barn to milk his cow early in the morning. He was milking away quietly and had the bucket almost half full when a bug flew into the barn and started circling his head. Suddenly, the bug flew into the cow's ear. The farmer didn't think much about it until the bug squirted out into his bucket. Looks like it went in one ear and out the udder. ☆

What goes bonk bonk bonk bonk bonk bonk?

A rubber-nosed clown falling down a flight of stairs.

SPOTLIGHT

Mike Myers

Is Mike Myers a great comedian? In the words of Austin Powers, one of his most famous characters, "Yeah, baby!"

Mike Myers grew up in Toronto, Ontario, Canada. He was first picked up on American radar in 1988, when he began his lengthy run on *Saturday Night Live*. Evidence of Myers's comedic creativity was clear in the memorable characters he created on *SNL:* Linda Richman, the "Coffee Talk" host based on Myers's own mother-in-law; Dieter, the spastic host of a European variety show called "Sprockets"; and, of course, Wayne Campbell, the host of "Wayne's World."

Myers and his *SNL* pal Dana Carvey took their "Wayne's World" skits to the big screen in 1992. The story of two heavy-metal geeks starring in a public-access cable show filmed in Wayne's basement, *Wayne's World* was a smash hit. Myers and Carvey followed with a sequel, *Wayne's World 2,* in 1993.

Myers spent the next few years perfecting a character he'd had in his mind for years—a spoof on the ultimate cinematic spy, James Bond. *Austin Powers: International Man of Mystery* hit theaters in 1997. Not a big box office hit, the movie raked in millions on video, becoming a cult sensation—and making Myers a household name. *Austin Powers: The Spy Who Shagged Me* emerged in 1999, cementing Myers's status as a comic genius.

While wit seemingly comes naturally to Myers, he has said he spends a long time developing characters and perfecting their mannerisms. Like any other profession, comedy requires hard work and persistence to succeed—and Myers is a perfect example of such determination.

BEHIND THE PUNCH LINE:
Impersonations

Have you ever heard someone with a funny voice on TV or in a movie, and then tried to mimic his or her voice? That's an *impersonation*. A comedian who is really talented at impersonations can often imitate not only someone's voice, but their gestures, their mannerisms, even their clothing style down to the last detail.

Comedians who do impersonations aren't trying to fool their audiences into believing that they actually are someone else, as an actor in a film might. It's more important to exaggerate things that make the other person so recognizable—a squeaky voice, hair twirling, a prop like a cane or a doll—than to nail the person's character exactly. It also helps to pick someone who is very famous, so the audience will be sure to get the joke. If the audience is just family, try imitating your big sister on the phone with her boyfriend or your mom talking to a client to get a bigger laugh.

Many famous comedians, like Robin Williams, have made careers out of their ability to impersonate others. Most skits on *Saturday Night Live* and other sketch comedy shows feature players who create characters based on real people. Try it, you'll like it!

Chuck goes in to his doctor and says, "Doctor, I'm a little embarrassed to talk about this, but I seem to be barfing a lot."

The doctor says, "Well, I'm glad you feel you can bring this up, Chuck." ☆

Why was the car smelly?

It had too much gas.

What animal is always getting food poisoning?

The yak.

Why did Tigger stick his head in the toilet?

He was looking for Pooh.

It was a beautiful summer in Sweden, and all the Swedish cows were enjoying excellent grass crops. There was more than enough grass to go around, and all through the fjords and dells you could hear the cows mooing with happiness. But some time in late July, there arrived a band of roughhousing moose who muscled the cows out of the way and began eating more grass than was seemingly possible. Then, just when it looked like things couldn't get worse, the moose started to throw up all over the place, nauseated from their grassy feasting. For the rest of the summer, the farmers could be heard complaining that "the hills are alive with the sounds of moose sick!" ☆

93

I zink I'm going to be Sick!

Silly Song

(Sung to the tune of "When the Saints Go Marching In")

Oh when the ants
Get in our food,
It puts us in an awful mood.
We find legs in our egg salad,
When the ants get in our food.

Oh when the dog
Drools on our meal,
To eat at all loses all appeal.
We find slobber on our sandwich,
When the dog drools on our meal.

Oh when the sand
Gets in our lunch,
Potato chips have extra crunch.
We find grit in ground-beef patties,
When the sand gets in our lunch.

94

Oh when the flies
Land on our spread,
We've no desire to be fed.
We find bugs on our bologna,
When the flies land on our spread.

Next time we dine
We'll stay inside.
Our hungry mouths we'll open wide.
Within walls, it's safe to swallow,
Next time we'll dine inside.

95

Another Silly Song

Everybody's doin' it, doin' it, doin' it;
Pickin' their noses and a-chewin' it.
You think it's some kinda candy
But it's snot.

What do you call a boy who's been half-eaten by a Python?

What do you call a dog with no legs? *Matt.*

What do you call a boy hanging on the wall? *Art.*

What do you call a boy floating in the pool? *Bob.*

What do you call a dog with a wooden leg? *Peg.*

What do you call a boy on stage? *Mike.*

What do you call a boy who's been mauled by a bear? *Gord.*

What do you call a boy who's been caught by a tribe of cannibals? *Stu.*

96

Les.

ROCKET SCIENCE

All the Mysteries of Outer Space, Made More Confusing

Darth Vader and Luke Skywalker were duking it out somewhere in space. Darth Vader said to Luke, "Join me and experience the power of the dark side!"

Luke replied, "The dark side can't be that powerful."

"Yes it is. I even know what you're getting for Christmas, Luke."

"How?" Luke asked.

"I felt your presents."

BZZZZT!..

WHOA! Thanks for the lightsaber, Darth-Dude! It even cuts through fruitcake!

Why did the earthling fall in love with the alien?

Because she was out of this world!

Why did Mr. Spock sneak into the ladies' room?

He wanted to go where no man had gone before.

Why did the atom cross the road?

Because it was time to split.

BEHIND THE PUNCH LINE:
The Funny Pages

When you read the comic strips every Sunday, do you think about the artists as comedians? Probably not—but they are. They use paper and pen rather than their voices and bodies to make people laugh.

Charles Schultz, who wrote "Peanuts" for fifty consecutive years until his death in 2000, managed to give each one of his characters a distinctly funny and different personality.

There was Charlie Brown, the eternally optimistic loser; Lucy, the grumpy meanie; Linus, who liked to be left alone; and Sally, the romantic, among others. Garry Trudeau, the author of "Doonesbury," uses his pen to poke fun at politics. "Dilbert" cartoonist Scott Anderson makes light of office jobs. And the list goes on.

What are your favorite comic strips? Next time you look at one, think about the artist applying the steps in this book in order to express a perfectly timed joke. You will see that comedy comes through in writing as well as it does in spoken words.

How can you tell if your dad's an alien?

He knows how to program the VCR.

How do you know when your little brother's an alien?

He can change TV channels from the sofa without using the remote.

How do you know when your older sister's an alien?

She always knocks before coming into your room.

What did the sun say when it was introduced to the earth?

"Pleased to heat you."

Hmm... perhaps something more in an exterior Latex...

A robot couple walks by a hardware store, and the female stops to admire the paint cans displayed in the window. "I'm sorry," says the male robot, "but your old coat will have to last you another year." ✩

What do you call a robot that always takes the longest route?

R2 Detour.

How did the scientist invent bug spray?

She started from scratch.

99

No driver's License, No License plate, No vehicle registration...

S herlock Holmes and his trusty associate Watson were on a camping trip. They had gone to bed and were lying there looking up at the sky. Holmes said, "Watson, look up and tell me what you see."

"Well, I see thousands of stars," he replied.

"And what does that tell you?" asked Holmes.

"I guess it means we're going to have another nice day tomorrow. What does it mean to you?"

"To me, it means that someone has stolen our tent." ✩

100

O ne day, a flying saucer lands in Times Square and tries to park in the middle of the sidewalk. Immediately a traffic cop rushes over to the Martian and says, "You can't park that thing here. Go find a legal spot."

The Martian looks up and says, "Take me to your meter." ✩

What did the alien say to the tabby cat?

"Take me to your litter."

What did the astronaut think of the takeoff?

She thought it was a blast.

How come aliens don't drown in hot chocolate?

They sit on the Mars-mallows.

Chris Rock

Chris Rock has gained fame as a sassy, wacky pop-culture expert. His witty commentary on current events has made him a comedy star for the MTV generation.

A teenage Rock was initiated into the Manhattan comedy club scene as a protégé of much-admired comic Eddie Murphy. Rock followed Murphy's career path to *Saturday Night Live,* where he appeared from 1990 to 1993.

Rock's comedy style has stayed true to Murphy's early style as well. He's raw and rebellious, but with a sophisticated edge that comes from closely watching the nightly news. He frequently tackles tough issues like race and poverty in his comedy routines and isn't afraid to make people angry to make a point.

After *SNL,* Rock produced several comedy specials that ran on the cable channel HBO. He has also appeared in several films, including *Lethal Weapon 4* (1998) and Eddie Murphy's feature flick *Dr. Doolittle* (1998).

Rock's frequent appearances on HBO and as host of several awards shows have created a solid fan base and cemented his status in the comedy world. However, he frequently protests that showbiz isn't going to his head.

Rock told *Esquire* magazine in 1997, "I'm not a superstar. Jim Carrey makes $20 million a movie. I make a weird face when they tell me I have to pay $8.50 to see one."

How do you know there's an alien in your house?

The TV gets better reception because of the extra antennae.

"I bet I can run faster than you can," one man bragged to the other.

"I bet you can't," the second man replied.

The two men went to the top of a 30-story building, and the first man leaned over and dropped his watch over the edge. In a whirl of dust, he raced down the stairs and moments later appeared at the ground level, reached out, and caught the watch before it hit the ground.

The second man nodded, smiled, and dropped his own watch over the edge. Taking his time, he strolled over to the elevator and pushed the button. On the way down he stopped at several floors, and when he finally reached the lobby he stopped to get a soda. He then calmly walked outside just in time to catch the falling watch.

"Hey, that was amazing!" said the first man, truly impressed. "How did you do that?"

"Simple," said the second man. "My watch is five minutes slow."

What did the alien say to the tree?

"Take me to your cedar."

HALLEY'S CANARY.

WATCH YOUR STEP

102

How do you throw the best bash in the universe?

Planet.

How do you get an astronaut's baby to fall asleep?

Rocket.

How does the man on the moon trim his hedge?

Eclipse it.

What sporting event do people from Venus, Mars, Saturn, and Mercury watch on TV every October?

The Out-of-This-World Series.

Why Is football so popular on Venus?

Because all the houses have Astroturf on their front lawns.

What's the best hockey team in the universe?

The All-Stars.

How did the astronaut feel when he ran into the alien with six lasers for arms?

Stunned.

Knock, knock.
Who's there?
Cosmos.
Cosmos who?
Cosmos of us are waiting outside, you should let us in!

163

...and I come in peace from Ear...

Tsk—You oxygen breathers are so annoying...

MNØBZZZT!

What's the difference between Neptune and Earth?

There's a world of difference!

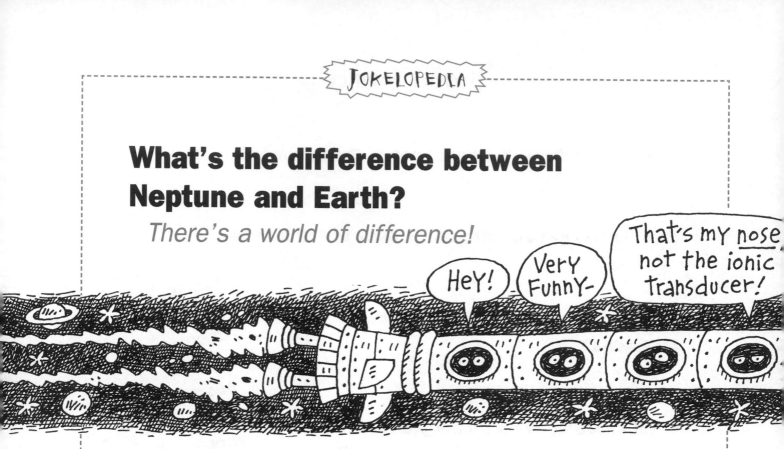

Hey!

Very Funny-

That's my <u>nose</u> not the ionic transducer!

164

How do astronauts take their kids to school?

In space station wagons.

What happens to astronauts who misbehave?

They're grounded.

What does an astronaut use to dust those hard-to-reach black holes?

A vacuum cleaner.

One astronaut asks another astronaut if he has ever heard of the planet Saturn. The second astronaut says, "I'm not sure, but it has a familiar ring." ☆

Helpful Hint

If anyone ever makes fun of you for wearing glasses, tell them you have a very high-tech titanium alloy detachable face and that you need the hooks in your glasses to keep your face attached to the rest of your head.

Why was the spacecraft reading the horoscopes?

It was a Gemini.

Norbert Lagenfeld was a mad scientist who was thought to be creating replicas of himself in his laboratory. This was making some of the townsfolk anxious, so they gathered whatever they could and proceeded up the hill to confront him. The town stationer was armed with a box of pens, the librarian with a pile of books, and a handful of farmers had heavy sacks of wheat slung over their shoulders.

When they got to Lagenfeld's mansion, they encountered dozens of replicas of the mad scientist running amok. The townsfolk set upon them, killing Lagenfeld's creations left and right. The stationer poked them to death with her pens, the librarian clobbered them over the head with his books. Meanwhile, the farmers were hitting the replicas with the sacks of wheat. Soon the townsfolk collapsed in exhaustion, their work done—but off in the distance they saw Lagenfeld himself jump into his car. The few farmers with any energy left heaved their bags toward the car, but the bags broke open harmlessly and Lagenfeld made his getaway. As he vanished into the distance, they could hear him cry: "Bics and tomes may break my clones, but grains will never harm me." ✪

105

How do you turn a regular scientist into a mad scientist?

Step on his toes.

How do you know when you're talking to a mad scientist and her clone?

They they say say everything everything twice twice.

What do you carve on a robot's tombstone?

Rust in peace.

How do spacemen hold up their pants?

With asteroid belts.

Why did the silly astronaut turn off all the lights on the spaceship?

He wanted to travel at the speed of dark.

What do you get when you cross a rocket ship with a potato?

Spudnik.

Knock, knock.
Who's there?
Apollo.
Apollo who?
Apollo-gize for not answering sooner!

FAMILY FUNNIES

Brothers, Sisters, and Aunts of Step-Uncles

DAD: When Abraham Lincoln was your age, he walked miles to school, uphill, in the snow, every day.
SON: Yeah? Well, when Abraham Lincoln was your age, Dad, he was president!

DAD 1: My son is so smart, I think he's more intelligent than the president.
DAD 2: Why do you say that?
DAD 1: Well, he could recite the Gettysburg Address when he was ten. Lincoln didn't recite it until he was fifty.

DAD: Today we celebrate Abraham Lincoln's birthday. Some people called him Honest Abe.
DAUGHTER: If he was so honest, then why do they close all the banks and keep kids home from school?

Four-score and seven years ago, or the polynomial inverse of the equivalent numerator, our forefathers...

What's the difference between a dog who sticks his head out the car window and your little brother or sister?

One's a neck in the pane, the other's a pain in the neck.

What did the pantyhose say to the nylons at the family reunion?

Wow, we really run in the family.

A little boy returned from the grocery store with his mom. While his mom put away the groceries, the little boy opened his box of animal crackers and spread them all over the kitchen table.

"What are you doing?" asked his mom.

"The box says you shouldn't eat them if the seal is broken," said the little boy. "I'm looking for the seal." ✡

A boy was riding in the elevator of a very tall building with his parents. He tugged on his father's coat and, when his father bent over, asked him a question.

The father frowned and shook his head. The little boy tugged on his father's coat again and asked the same question.

"No," said the father.

When the little boy tugged on his father's coat a third time, the father lost his patience and said, "I don't care how Superman does it! We're going up this way!" ✡

The daughter of a famous basketball star was watching television and her mom was in the other room. "Mommy, come here! Daddy's on the television again!" yelled the little girl.

Her mom yelled back, "You just tell Daddy to get off the television and sit in his armchair like a normal adult." ☆

A mom walks into a store and asks if she could have a Pokémon game for her daughter. The store clerk replies, "I'm sorry, ma'am, but we don't do exchanges." ☆

What's it called when you stop the car and make your annoying sibling get out?

A pest stop.

A little girl became ill and was taken to the hospital. It was her first time away from home and she began to cry. The nurse was concerned and asked the little girl if she was homesick.

"No,"said the girl. "I'm *here* sick!" ☆

Mary's husband lost his job as a tailor in a local shop, but he didn't talk much about it. He didn't seem to be too bothered, though, and Mary was so curious that she finally asked, "Why is it that you're not working as a tailor anymore, Bill?"

Bill thought a moment and then he said, "Well, I guess it didn't really suit me. It was a sew-sew job." ☆

110

"I am going to be a famous magician," said Eddie to his father, "because I can make a golf ball float."

Eddie's father was very curious. "And how do you do that?" he asked.

Hmm—that vanilla's pretty thick—better get my nine iron...

"Well, it's very scientific. It requires some magic ingredients," said Eddie.

Eddie's father leaned forward in his chair. "Oh, really," he said. "And what are they?"

"Well, the golf ball, of course. And then two scoops of ice cream and some root beer." ☆

BEHIND THE PUNCH LINE:
Vaudeville

Vaudeville is a French word meaning a popular, comic song. The term eventually came to mean a comedy show featuring a collection of variety acts—singers as well as dancers, acrobats, comedians, mimes, ventriloquists, and performing animals. Skits and short plays were also part of the elaborate shows.

Vaudeville was one of the most popular forms of entertainment during the early part of the twentieth century. In 1919, there were more than 900 theaters in the country featuring vaudeville shows. At that time, movies were still new and they had no sound, since no one had figured out how to combine sounds with the pictures yet. Most working actors of that time performed in vaudeville shows. However, as new technology came along, "talkies"—movies with sound—appeared and became very popular. They became so popular that vaudeville shows were kicked out of their theaters to make room for movie screens.

It is a shame that live theater like vaudeville became less popular as the movie industry grew larger. Vaudeville shows allowed actors to interact with the audience and to see firsthand what made the fans laugh. If a part of the show wasn't funny, it could be replaced with something else, so no two shows were exactly the same.

A dad goes into a pet store and asks if he can return the puppy he got for his son. The owner replied, "I'm sorry, sir, but we've already sold your son to someone else."

A man was walking across a bridge when he noticed a little boy crying. He went over to the boy and asked him what was the matter. The boy wailed, "My sandwich fell into the water!"

"It must have been a delicious sandwich," said the man. "Was it with bologna and cheese?"

"No," sobbed the little boy. By this time, the boy was crying a lot and the man was beginning to worry.

"Well, was it with just cheese?" asked the man.

"No," cried the boy. "It was with my brother!" ☆

Little Sally always looked forward to her lunch, but today Sally's mom was excited about the new treat she had planned for Sally. Sally's mom set down a carefully arranged plate on the table and then went to the kitchen to get some napkins. She was completely confused when she came back to see Sally crying at the table.

"What's wrong, Sally? Don't you like the animal crackers I bought for you?" asked her mom.

Sally just cried even harder and wailed, "But Mommy, we're vegetarians!" ☆

How did the giant's wife know that Jack was coming?

She could hear Jack and the beans talk!

A teenager tells his father, "There's trouble with the car. It has water in the carburetor."

The father looks confused and says, "Water in the carburetor? That's ridiculous."

But the son insists. "I tell you the car has water in the carburetor."

His father is starting to get a little nervous. "You don't even know what a carburetor is," he says. "I'll check it out. Where's the car?"

"In the pool." ☆

Two mothers were comparing stories about their children. The first one complained that her son never wanted to get out of bed in the morning. The second told her, "I don't have that problem. When it's time for my son to get up, I just throw the cat in his bed."

"How does that help?" asked the first mom.

"He sleeps with the dog." ☆

113

A little boy was practicing the violin in the living room while his mother was trying to read in the den. The family dog was lying in the den, and as the screeching sounds of the violin reached the dog's ears, he began to howl loudly. The mother listened to the dog and the violin for as long as she could. Then she jumped up, dropped her paper to the floor, and shouted above the noise, "For goodness' sake, can't you play something the dog doesn't know?" ☆

...and to interpret Mozart correctly, one must play from the heart!

114

A father and his small daughter were standing in front of the tiger's cage at the zoo. Dad was explaining how ferocious and strong tigers are, and the little girl was listening to him with a very serious expression.

"Daddy," she said finally, "if the tiger got out of his cage and ate you up . . ."

"Yes, dear?" asked the father.

"Which bus would I take home?" ☆

The Marx Brothers

The Marx Brothers were a comedy team of brothers—Groucho, Chico, Harpo, Gummo, and Zeppo—who first gained notice for their use of improvisation onstage. The brothers were organized into an act in 1914 by their mother, who often performed with them in vaudeville shows. The brothers (except for Gummo, who quit the act in 1924 and was replaced by younger brother Zeppo) appeared on Broadway in 1924 in a show called *I'll Say She Is.* During the show, the Marx Brothers made up most of their lines on the spot and even talked to the audience from the stage; they rarely used the script. People attended the show over and over because no two performances were ever alike.

The brothers' first film, *The Cocoanuts,* was created from another Broadway show. It opened in 1929, and the Marx Brothers immediately became movie stars. During the 1930s, they made a movie a year. Movies like *Animal Crackers, Duck Soup,* and *A Night at the Opera* showcased the Marxes' flawless comic timing. Although the brothers were not able to improvise as much in films as they did onstage, their easy interaction with one another on the movie screen made it seem as if they were.

THE MARX BROS.
"ROOM SERVICE"
LUCILLE BALL
ANN MILLER
FRANK ALBERTSON

A man bought his wife a talking bird for her birthday. It spoke seven languages and cost him a month's pay. "Well," he asked her when he got home, "did you get the bird I sent you?"

"Yes," answered his wife. "I already have it in the oven."

"What! That bird could speak seven languages!" said the man, upset.

"Then why didn't it say anything?" ✩

What do you get when you cross your brother with an owl?

A wise guy.

116

Why did Billy's brother run to the refrigerator when Billy asked him to play?

Because his favorite game was freeze tag.

One day a little girl put her shoes on by herself for the first time. Her mother noticed that her left shoe was on her right foot.

"Honey," said the mom, "I think your shoes are on the wrong feet."

The little girl looked up and said, "No, Mom, I *know* these are my feet." ✩

A telemarketer calls a house and a little boy answers. The little boy whispers, "Hello?"

The salesman says, "Yes, can I speak to your mommy?"

"No," the little boy whispers. "She's busy."

The salesman then says, "Okay, can I speak to your daddy, please?"

"He's busy, too," the little boy whispers.

Starting to get annoyed, the salesman says, "All right, is there another adult in the house?"

"Yes," the boy again whispers. "There's a policeman."

"A policeman?!" the salesman gasps. "Can I speak to him?"

"No," whispers the boy. "He's busy, too."

As a last resort, the salesman asks one last time, "Okay, are there any *other* adults there?"

"Yes," whispers the boy. "There's a fireman."

"A fireman!" exclaims the salesman. "Can I speak to him?"

"No," whispers the boy. "He's busy, too."

"Little boy," says the salesman, "with all of those adults in the house, what are they busy doing?"

After a short pause the little boy whispers, "Looking for me." ✤

Why do women have to carry babies?

Because babies aren't big enough to carry their mothers.

118

Little Doris went to visit the new baby at the Johnsons' house. Mrs. Johnson answered the door and Doris said, "Hi, Mrs. Johnson, is baby Bobby there? Could I talk to him?"

Mrs. Johnson smiled and said, "I'm sorry but Bobby is only a little baby. He can't talk yet."

Doris said, "That's OK, I'll wait." ✩

What did the paint give the wall on their first anniversary?

A new coat.

Why did the pregnant woman race to the hospital?

She wanted to have a speedy delivery.

When should you bring your father to class?

When you have a pop quiz.

"Are caterpillars good to eat?" asked a little boy at the dinner table.

"No," said his father. "What makes you ask a question like that?"

"You had one on your salad, but it's gone now." ☆

Why was the margarine unhappy when she gave birth to the marmalade?

She was expecting something butter.

Jack couldn't mow the lawn yesterday because he sprained his ankle. What do you think his dad said to that?

"That's a lame excuse!"

119

PRACTICAL JOKE

Tell someone that you can pin a glass of water to the wall. Naturally, your victim will not believe you, so you set out to prove it. You will need a glass (a real glass, not a paper cup) of water and a straight pin. Hold the glass up and start pinning it up—then drop the pin. Ask your victim very nicely to please pick up the pin for you. When he or she bends over to get the pin, pour the water on his or her head.

Mikey's parents were going out, and Mikey said, "For twenty bucks, Dad, I'll be good."

"Oh, please," said his father. "When I was your age, I was good for nothing." ✫

There was once a young prince in a faraway land who was very much loved by his parents. The king and queen would take him to the circus and feed him all the cakes and pies he wanted. When the prince got a little older, however, he started to rebel. He hung around with the wrong subjects and would stray far from the castle on his own. One day, he was ambushed by an evil warlock in the forest who changed him into a fool. The courtiers made fun of him and his parents sent him into exile. What's the moral of the story?

Heir today, goon tomorrow. ✫

120

Be Gone, Ye Jerk!

'Tis a shame, but Ye still have me!

Three old men have just arrived in heaven and are attending an orientation meeting. They are all asked, "When you are at the funeral and your friends and families are mourning, what would you like to hear them say about you?"

The first guy says, "I'd like to hear them say that I was a great doctor and a great family man."

The second guy says, "I would like them to say that I was a wonderful husband and schoolteacher, and that I made a huge difference in our children of tomorrow."

The last guy thinks a moment and says, "I think I'd like to hear them say 'Look! He's moving!'" ☆

A bully is picking on a boy's sister. The boy runs up and pushes the bully away, saying, "Stop picking on my sister—that's my job!" ☆

When do mothers have baby boys?
On son days.

What do weathermen call their baby boys?
Sunny.

Do you know that robot?
No, I haven't met him, but I'm friends with his tran-sister.

Why did the little girl bury her father and mother?
She wanted to grow a family tree.

A man and his wife were driving their RV across the country and were nearing a town called Kissimmee. They noted the strange spelling and tried to figure out how to pronounce it: KISS-i-me, kiss-I-me, kiss-i-ME. They grew more and more confused as they drove into the town. Because they were hungry, they pulled into a restaurant to get something to eat. At the counter, the man said to the server: "My wife and I can't figure out how to pronounce the name of this place. Will you tell me where we are and say it very slowly so that I can understand?"

The server looked at him and said: "Buuurrrgerrrr Kiiiinnnng." ☆

SPLORT!

122

What's the matter—don't you understand plain English?

Objects of Amusement

Household Items Unite

What did one plate say to the other?

"Dinner's on me."

What did one wall say to the other?

"Meet me at the corner."

Why couldn't the tire quit its job?

It was flat broke.

Why did the kid throw quarters under the car wheel?

He wanted to help change a tire.

Why did the stoplight turn red?

Wouldn't you if you had to change in the middle of the street?

Aaah! You're a cake and ice cream MESS, young man! You just march yourself into the dishwasher this instant!

What's the difference between a red light and a green light?

The color, silly!

What did one toilet say to the other?

What's the difference between a summer dress in winter and a pulled molar?

One is too thin, the other tooth out.

What's the difference between an old penny and a new dime?

Nine cents.

What has one horn and gives milk?

A milk truck.

124

Why do refrigerators hum?

Because they don't know the words.

Did you hear the one about the knives?

It's a cutup.

Did you hear about the jigsaw puzzle that got fired?

It went to pieces.

You look a little flushed!

WAYS TO DESCRIBE A NOT-SO-SMART PERSON

(they'll never know it's an insult!):

Not the sharpest knife in the drawer.

Not the sharpest tool in the shed.

Not the brightest bulb on the Christmas tree.

(S)he fell out of the stupid tree and hit all the branches on the way down.

One fry shy of a Happy Meal.

A few sandwiches short of a picnic.

A few sodas short of a six-pack.

A few grapes short of a bunch.

The wheel is spinning, but the hamster's dead.

The butter has slipped off his/her pancake.

The antenna isn't picking up all the channels.

The elevator doesn't go all the way to the top.

There! The holes should make me lighter!

Did you hear about the ice that got fired?

It was crushed.

Did you hear about the underwear that got fired?

It was bummed.

What do you put in a barrel to make it lighter?

A hole.

Why are lost things always in the last place you looked?

Because when you find them, you stop looking.

What did the rope say after it tangled?

"Oh no, knot again!"

Why couldn't the bell keep a secret?

It always tolled.

What climbs trees without a sound, and has feet that always touch the ground?

A vine.

What has teeth but doesn't bite?

A comb.

What has a head and a tail but no body?

A coin!

NEW SHOELACE: Why are you crying, Old Shoelace? Can't you tie a bow?
OLD SHOELACE: No, I'm a frayed knot.

Why did the boy eat the lamp?

His mother told him to have a light snack.

ha-ha!

What is a soda machine's favorite dance?

The can-can!

127

What do you throw out when you need it, and take in when you don't need it?

An anchor.

What driver never speeds?

A screwdriver!

To heck with the speed limit! Get this belt sander moving before the hardware store finds out we're gone!

OFF ON CLICK!

OK-hand over all your cushions, Sofa-boy! C'mon-I ain't got all day!

Why was the couch afraid of the chair?
The chair was armed.

128

What did the bald man say when he got a comb for his birthday?
"I'll never part with it."

What kind of hat does Sir Lancelot wear?
A knight cap.

What did the 0 say to the 8?
"Nice belt."

How can you get four suits for a dollar?
Buy a deck of cards.

Why shouldn't you hang a funny picture on your wall?
The plaster might crack up.

What did the lightbulb say to the switch?
"You turn me on."

Janeane Garofalo

Janeane Garofalo is the ultimate smart person's comedian—right down to the THINK tattoo on her arm. She's bold, brash, and unafraid to tell anyone exactly what's on her mind. Yet Garofalo has achieved the most success playing characters who lack self-confidence. Many of her characters put themselves down to get others to laugh. Garofalo's brand of scornful, sarcastic comedy has earned her many fans over the years.

Beginning her career as a stand-up comic, Garofalo's role on the HBO series *The Larry Sanders Show* was what got her noticed by Hollywood. Garofalo's first major film role was in *Reality Bites,* directed by her friend Ben Stiller. Garofalo had appeared on Stiller's short-lived MTV sketch comedy show *The Ben Stiller Show* a few years earlier and the two became fast friends. They are still close; they even published a book together called *Feel This Book,* a self-help parody, in 1999.

The Truth About Cats and Dogs (1996) was Garofalo's next big hit. The film, featuring Garofalo as a radio talk-show veterinarian so insecure that she persuades her neighbor to pose as her on a date, was a lesson in learning to be yourself— very similar to Garofalo's own offscreen philosophy.

Janeane doesn't shy away from talking about her own insecurities and fears, nor is she fearful of tackling tough topics like dieting and Hollywood rejection in the press. She's real and honest, and she brings these traits to life in her screen characters.

What did the recliner say to her son?

"You're such a La-Z-Boy."

What did the couch say halfway through the marathon?

Sofa, so good.

What did the carpet say to the floor?

"Don't move, I've got you covered."

A man is locked in a room with no way to get out. In the room there is a piano, a saw, a table, and a baseball bat. How could he get out?

He could take a key from the piano and unlock the door.

He could take the bat and get three strikes. Then he'd be out.

He could take the saw and cut the table in two. Then by putting the two halves together, he would have a "hole" and he could get out. ☆

What do you call an angle that's gotten into a car crash?

A rectangle.

What does purple do when it gets angry?

It sees red.

Why isn't red happy to see purple?

It starts to feel blue.

130

What kind of bow is impossible to tie?

A rainbow.

How did the desk calendar snub the inkwell?

She wouldn't give him a date.

Why are riddles like pencils?

They're no good unless they have a point!

What happens when you annoy a clock?

It gets ticked off!

What happens when you throw a clock in the air?

Time's up!

131

What did the big clock say to his shy son?

"Take your hands off your face."

Why did Bobby tie a clock to his palms?

He wanted to have time on his hands.

Why did the cabinet go to the psychiatrist?

It kept talking to its shelf.

...and all day LONG, it's dishes IN, dishes OUT! SLAM! SLAM! SLAM!

Yes...und you are starting to get a <u>handle</u> on zis problem?

A genius was working on a new invention. It was such a great machine that it could perform twenty tasks at once. It could water a garden, pour milk, sew buttons on a coat, scrub dishes, squirt ketchup, walk the dog, solve math problems, catch flies, bake cakes, stamp envelopes and lick them shut, find lost keys, tie shoelaces, change a baby's diaper, play dodge ball, fold laundry, make hot-fudge sundaes, clean the cat's litter box, turn on the radio, plant petunias, and answer the phone. The genius had all the parts laid out in front of him, but needed something to put the machine together. So he sent his dumb assistant to the store to buy some glue. The store had almost everything—toothpaste, vacuum cleaners, cream soda, breaded halibut, licorice, but no glue. The assistant wasn't upset. He just bought the breaded halibut.

132

How come?

It doesn't take a genius to know fish sticks. ✫

What happens to spoons who work too much?

They go stir-crazy.

Why did the watch go on vacation?
To unwind.

Marcia asked Bill, "Was that the clock tocking earlier?"
"Not to me," said Bill. "It wouldn't even give me the time of day."

THE MAKING OF A COMEDIAN

Step 4: Plotting Your Strategy

If you were able to convince someone to buy you this book, you've mastered the first principle of joke telling: strategy. Strategy is one of the most important tools in the comedian's box of tricks. It's how you plan your act to make people laugh when you want them to laugh.

The secret to influencing others is to have confidence in yourself. You are the one onstage, under the spotlight—you have the power. So don't apologize before you tell a joke—especially one that comes from this book.

133

How do you keep a window from getting cold?

Shutter.

What accidents happen every 24 hours?

Day breaks and night falls.

Did you hear about the crimes over at that house they're renovating?

The shower was stalled while the curtains were held up. Apparently the doors were also hung, and I heard the window was framed for it. ☆

Ooh... that smarts!

You're telling me...

What made the newspaper blush?

It saw the comic strip.

Why was the dresser embarrassed?

Its drawers fell down.

Why was the nail so unhappy?

The carpenter kept hitting it on the head.

What nail does a carpenter hate to hit?

His thumbnail.

Why was the flight late?

It forgot its staircase.

What did the refrigerator say to the milk?

"Now, don't get fresh with me."

Randy and Matt set out for a four-day hike in the desert, carrying all their supplies. Matt noticed that Randy was lugging a heavy car door and asked him why. Randy replied: "So that when I get hot I can roll down the window." ☆

What did the sink say to the dirty dishes?

"You're in hot water now!"

The washer-and-dryer salesman says to the customer, "Have you decided on a model?"

"I'm not sure," says the customer.

The salesman says, "That's no problem—just take it for a spin." ☆

What did the milk say to the blender?

"I'm all shook up."

Why was the saucepan always getting in trouble?

It was too hot to handle.

Mrs. Gumbo was backing out of her driveway when she heard a thump. She stopped the car in a panic and rushed out to see what had happened. There, at the end of the driveway, was a small dog lying on its side. It was dead. Mrs. Gumbo felt awful. She knew it was her neighbor's dog. Looking very worried, she climbed the front stairs of her neighbor's house and knocked on the door. She waited for a couple of minutes. Finally, a tall man answered.

"I'm so sorry," Mrs. Gumbo said. "I was backing out of my driveway just a few minutes ago when I heard a thump. I got out of the car to see what had happened. Your dog was lying dead at the end of the driveway. I'm afraid that I ran over her and I feel terrible about it. I insist on replacing her."

The tall man paused and then said, "Well, I guess you can bring me my slippers and newspaper tomorrow morning." ☆

135

Why did the teapot blush?

She thought the kettle was whistling at her.

What did the soda say to the bottle opener?

"Hey, can you help me find my pop?"

MUFFY: Sir, can you please call me a taxi?
DOORMAN: Certainly, dear. You are a taxi.

Why was the pantry so good at telling the future?

It knew what was in store.

What did the broom say to the dustpan?

"Let's make a clean sweep."

Why does the toast like the knife?

Because the knife butters him up.

If a nut on a wall is a walnut, what is a nut in the bathroom?

A pee can.

PEPPER SHAKER: Why won't the salt shaker shake out any salt?
KETCHUP BOTTLE: I suppose it goes against the grain.

What do you get when you cross a bed with a kitchen appliance?

A four-poster toaster.

136

ha-ha!

Truly TASTELESS JOKES

Food Strikes Back

CUSTOMER: What is this insect in my soup?
WAITER: I wish you wouldn't ask me.
I don't know one bug from another.

LITTLE GIRL: I'm thirsty.
LITTLE BOY: I'm Friday.
Come over Saturday and
we'll have a sundae.

CUSTOMER: Do you
serve crabs here?

WAITER: We serve
everyone. Sit right down.

I'LL have the fish.

Would you like seaweed with that?

Did you hear about the farmer arrested for selling rotten fruit?

He was judged by his pears.

Why did the cucumber need a lawyer?

It was in a pickle.

138

PRACTICAL JOKE

Ways to torment the pizza guy:

Ask for the crust on top this time.

Ask if you get to keep the pizza box when you're done. When they say yes, act very relieved.

Pretend like you know the person on the phone from somewhere. Say something like, "Hey, your voice sounds familiar . . . I think we went to bed-wetters camp together about five years ago!"

Make the first topping you order pepperoni. Just before you hang up, say, "Remember—no pepperoni, please!" Don't wait for a response.

If the person on the other end gets annoyed with you, say, "The last guy let me do it!"

Why do nuns like Swiss cheese the best?

Because it's hole-y.

Why did the chocolate milk win the race?

It was Quik.

Why did the strawberry need a lawyer?

It was in a jam.

Why didn't the prawn share his dessert?

He was shellfish.

139

Why is monastery food so greasy?

It's all cooked by friars.

What did the mama melon say to her daughter when the girl wanted to run away and marry her boyfriend?

You canteloupe.

If you eat three-quarters of a pie, what do you have?

An angry parent!

Did you hear the one about the compulsive liar sandwich?

It was full of baloney.

What goes best with toast when you're in a car?

Traffic jam.

What's big and white and lives on Mars?

A martian-mallow.

Why are raspberries such bad drivers?

They're always getting into jams.

140

What did the cucumber say to the vinegar?

"Well, this is a fine pickle you've gotten us into!"

Why was the mushroom the hit of the party?

He was a fungi.

What has lots of eyes but can't see?

A potato!

How does broccoli feel when it's been cooked?

It's steamed.

BART: I feel like spaghetti.
HOWARD: Funny, you don't look like spaghetti!

Adam Sandler

Adam Sandler is a multitalented comedian whose zany onstage persona recalls that of his comic heroes Rodney Dangerfield and Cheech and Chong. In reality, however, Sandler doesn't drink, doesn't do drugs, and is so close to his parents that he called one of his comedy albums *Stan and Judy's Kid* in their honor.

Sandler was first noticed during his five-year stint on *Saturday Night Live,* the popular comedy sketch show on NBC. From 1990 to 1995, Sandler portrayed characters like Opera Man. It was on *SNL* that Sandler began writing and performing original songs, like his wildly popular "Chanukah Song," "Lunchlady Land," and "Red Hooded Sweatshirt." These and other songs appear on Sandler's four comedy albums.

It wasn't long before Hollywood began calling Sandler's name. Sandler had appeared in a few feature films while on *SNL,* but it was his portrayal of a goofy kid forced to repeat all twelve grades in order to receive his inheritance in 1995's *Billy Madison* that cemented his name in moviegoers' minds. Sandler followed with a turn as a hockey-player-turned-golfer in *Happy Gilmore* (1996) and a benchwarmer-turned-football-hero in *The Waterboy* (1998). Lately, his fans have seen the softer side of Sandler in such flicks as *The Wedding Singer* (1998), in which he plays the part of a singer who is smitten with Drew Barrymore, and *Big Daddy* (1999), in which he tries to adopt a little boy to impress his girlfriend.

Incidentally, the same group of New York University buddies who helped Sandler write the comedy routines that he performed in New York and Boston clubs and on the college circuit now help him write his movies! Sandler's multimedia success is proof of a winning combination of wackiness and warm fuzziness.

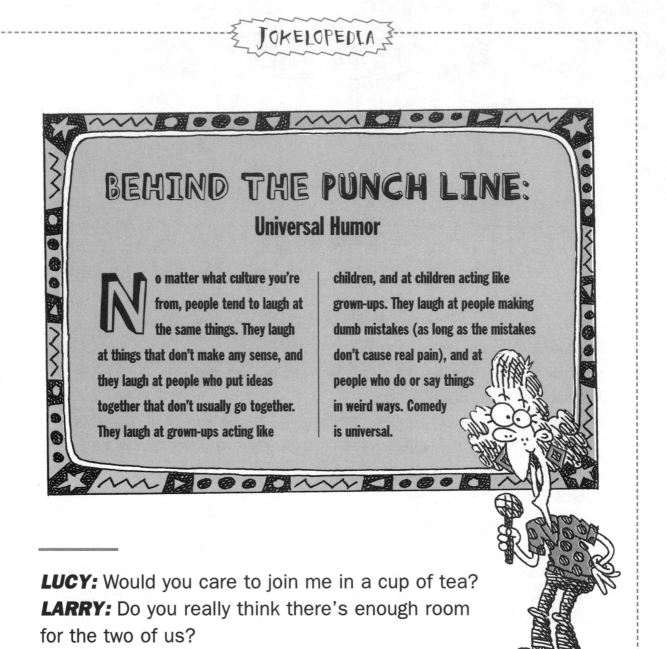

BEHIND THE PUNCH LINE:
Universal Humor

No matter what culture you're from, people tend to laugh at the same things. They laugh at things that don't make any sense, and they laugh at people who put ideas together that don't usually go together. They laugh at grown-ups acting like children, and at children acting like grown-ups. They laugh at people making dumb mistakes (as long as the mistakes don't cause real pain), and at people who do or say things in weird ways. Comedy is universal.

142

LUCY: Would you care to join me in a cup of tea?
LARRY: Do you really think there's enough room for the two of us?

A woman sits down in a restaurant and says to the waiter, "Waiter, I'd like an alligator, and make it snappy."

Robbie and his friends were talking after school. "Where's your favorite place to eat a hamburger?" asked Owen. Jimmy said he liked to sit in the park. Sam said he liked the picnic tables at the fair. "What about you, Robbie?" Owen asked. "Where's your favorite place to eat a hamburger?" Robbie replied, "In my mouth." ✩

CUSTOMER: Waiter, my vegetables just punched me!
WAITER: That's because they're black-eyed peas.

CUSTOMER: Waiter, there's a jack in my soup!
WAITER: That's because we made it with bean stock.

CUSTOMER: Why are there antlers on my filet mignon?
WAITER: Sorry, sir, that must be a moose steak.

CUSTOMER: Waiter, there's a fly in my alphabet soup!
WAITER: That's no fly, that's a spelling bee.

CUSTOMER: Waiter, there's a fly in my soup!
WAITER: Shhh, you're making the other customers jealous.

CUSTOMER: Waiter, there's a fly in my soup!
WAITER: Don't worry, sir, we won't charge you extra for it.

CUSTOMER: Waiter, what's this fly doing in my soup?
WAITER: Looks like he's drowning, ma'am.

CUSTOMER: Waiter, there's a fly doing the breaststroke in my soup!
WAITER: You're mistaken, sir. That's the butterfly.

CUSTOMER: Yesterday there wasn't a fly in my soup, but tonight there is one!
WAITER: That's because we're a fly-by-night operation, sir.

Look—we know it was YOU! Your sesame seeds were found at the scene!

144

What did the police do with the hamburger?

They grilled him.

Why do blue cheeses look alike?

They're all cut from the same mold.

What do blue cheese and a nose have in common?

They can both smell and be runny.

Why was the water fountain taken to court?

For being drunk in a public place.

Why did the woman divorce the grape?

She was tired of raisin' kids.

What did the grape say when the rhinoceros trampled it?

Not much. It just let out a little wine.

Why did the insect collector toss the butter dish across the restaurant?

He wanted to see the butter fly.

What did the TV dinner say after it had been packaged?

"Curses, foiled again!"

Why did the Rice Krispies go Snap, Quackle, Pop?

Crackle ducked out.

Why did the egg accuse the chef of cruelty?

He put her in a bowl and beat her.

What kind of exercises do pancakes do?

Jumping flapjacks.

Where do lettuces practice law?

At the salad bar.

How do you make a casserole?

Put it on a skateboard.

145

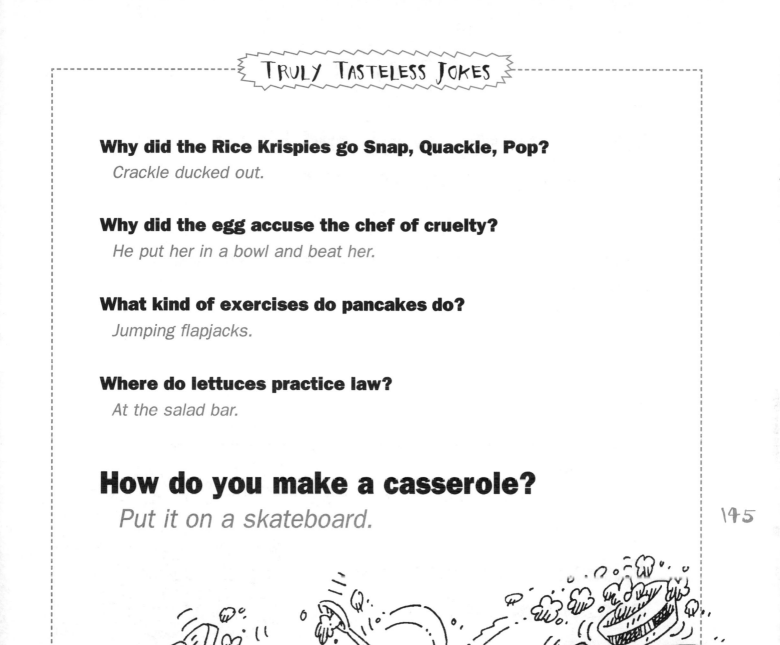

What did the gardener say to the vegetables?

"Lettuce, turnip, and pea."

Why did the other vegetables like the corn?

He was always willing to lend an ear.

When is a carton of milk like rain?

When it pours.

What's small, round, and blue?

A cranberry holding its breath.

What did the Martian say when his spaceship landed at Taco Bell?

"Take me to the big enchilada."

What should you do if your cake strikes out?

Call in the next batter.

Why did the salad make the chef turn around?

She didn't want him to see her dressing.

(Sigh) When I'm with you, time just slips away...

TUNNEL OF LOVE

What do you call two banana peels?

A pair of slippers.

Why did the mama bread get mad at the papa bread?

He was always loafing around.

What do you get when you cross an ear of corn with a spider?

Cob webs.

What did the corn give his fiancée when he proposed?

An ear ring.

146

A broccoli, a tomato, and a yam were running in a race. The broccoli got off to a great start, but being a green runner, didn't have the strength to finish the race. The yam and the tomato were neck and neck for the first stretch, but the tomato quickly fell behind. The yam was about to reach the end of the track, but collapsed in exhaustion right before the finish line. Over the course of an hour, the tomato ran the entire length of the race, and won.

Why was the tomato so successful?

The tomato paste itself. ✩

Why didn't the salad joke make it into the book?

It got tossed.

147

What do you get when you cross chocolate powder with a magic dragon?

Cocoa Puffs.

Why didn't the man fix dinner?

Because people always say "If it ain't broke, don't fix it!"

Do you have pig's feet?

Then how come you're walking like that?

ha-ha!

Do you have a head of lettuce?

Then how come your face is so green?

Why couldn't the monkey catch the banana?

The banana split.

What did the cookie say to the melon?

Nothing. Cookies can't talk, silly!

Try this everyday play on words.

Say your brother asks you to make him a peanut butter sandwich. What do you say? Pretend you're a genie who has the power to transform!

YOUR BROTHER: Could you make me a peanut butter sandwich?
YOU: Abracadabra! There, you're a peanut butter sandwich.

The same gag works for other types of sandwiches, chocolate cakes, and cups of tea. This joke is good for a few laughs, but don't do it too often or someone might start playing tricks on you!

148

ha-ha!

ha-ha!

ha-ha!

SHOWBIZ SHENANIGANS

Games with Famous Names

Which movie director always forgets to wear sunblock?

Steven Peelberg.

What gets Jackie Chan sick every winter?

Kung flu.

What did Bugs Bunny say to Michael Jordan?

"Eh . . . what's up, jock?"

Who is Superman's most religious enemy?

Lex Lutheran.

Eh...what's up, jock?

Mary Poppins moved to California and started a business telling people's fortunes. But she doesn't read palms or tea leaves, she smells a person's breath. The sign outside reads: "Super California Mystic, Expert Halitosis." ☆

What was Snow White told when it took longer to develop her photos than she was expecting?

"Don't worry, some day your prints will come."

How did Mary, Mary, Quite Contrary make her garden grow?

With water, silly.

Skipper was always bragging to his boss, "You know, I know everyone there is to know. Just name someone, anyone, and I know them." One day, tired of Skipper's boasting, his boss calls his bluff. "Okay, Skipper, how about Tom Cruise?"

"Sure, yes, Tom and I are old friends, and I can prove it." So Skipper and his boss fly out to Hollywood and knock on Tom Cruise's door, and sure enough, Tom Cruise shouts, "Skipper! Great to see you! You and your friend come right in and join me for lunch!"

Although impressed, Skipper's boss is still skeptical. After they leave Cruise's house, he tells Skipper that he thinks it was just lucky that Skipper knew Cruise.

"Go ahead, name anyone else," Skipper says.

"The president of the United States," his boss quickly replies.

"Yes," Skipper says, "I know him. Let's fly out to Washington." And off they go. As they tour the White House, the president spots Skipper and motions him and his boss over, saying, "Skipper, what a surprise! I was just on my way to a meeting, but you and your friend come on in and let's have a cup of coffee first and catch up." Well, the boss is very shaken by now, but still not totally convinced. After they leave the White House grounds, he expresses his doubts to Skipper, who again tells him to name anyone else.

"The Pope," his boss suggests.

"Sure!" says Skipper. "My family is very religious, and I've known the Pope a long time." So off they fly to Rome. Skipper and his boss are assembled with the masses in Vatican Square when Skipper says, "This will never work. I can't catch the Pope's eye among all these people. Tell you what—I know all the guards, so let me just go upstairs and I'll come out on the balcony with the Pope." And he disappears into the crowd headed toward the Vatican. Sure enough, half an hour later Skipper emerges with the Pope on the balcony. But when Skipper returns, he finds that his boss has had a heart attack and is surrounded by paramedics. Making his way to his boss's side, Skipper asks him, "What happened?"

His boss looks up and says, "I was doing fine until you and the Pope came out on the balcony and the man next to me said, 'Who's that on the balcony with Skipper?'" ☆

151

The TV game show was really close. One contestant was just 200 points behind the leader and the host was just about to ask him the final question, worth 500 points!

"To be today's champion," the host said, "name two of Santa's reindeer."

The contestant gave a sigh, relieved that he had drawn such an easy question. "Rudolph!" he said confidently. "And Olive!"

The audience in the TV studio started to applaud (there was a little sign above their heads that told them to clap), but the applause quickly faded into mumbling. The confused host replied, "Yes, we'll accept Rudolph, but could you please explain Olive?"

The man looked impatiently at the host and said, "You know: 'Olive, the other reindeer, used to laugh and call him names . . .'"

Darn! Not again!

What stands in New York, holds a torch, and sneezes a lot?
The Ah-Choo of Liberty.

How do the three men in the tub sign their love letters?
"I lub-a-dub-dub you."

What do you call a little blue man who lives on the West Coast?
Papa Surf.

Gesundheit! **What do you get when you cross Mickey's girlfriend with a shrinking machine?**
Mini Mouse.

How did Minnie Mouse save Mickey from drowning?

She gave him mouse-to-mouse resuscitation.

How do you make a Rolling Stone?

Push a rock down a hill.

What did the Lone Ranger say after he was thrown from his horse?

"I've fallen and I can't giddyup."

Once upon a time, the Norse god Loki played a nasty trick on a mortal named Inga. Loki told Inga that if she married an ugly man named Sven, stayed with him for three years, and then threw him into the ocean, a beautiful fur coat that would keep Inga warm through the difficult winters would rise out of the water. So Inga married Sven and stayed with him for three awful years. Then she took him out on the ocean and threw him overboard. A few minutes later, a coat rose out of the ocean, but it wasn't a beautiful coat, like Inga was expecting. It was a horrid, threadbare coat made out of muskrat, three sizes too small. Inga cried to the heavens: "Loki! You lied to me!"

And Loki replied: "You've learned two important lessons, Inga. One: don't marry for riches. And two: you can lead a Norse to water, but you can't make him mink." ☆

If George Washington went to Washington wearing a white winter coat while his wife waited in Wilmington, how many Ws are there in all?

None. There are no Ws in "all."

153

What did the captain of the *Titanic* say when his first mate asked if things were going to get worse?

"This is just the tip of the iceberg."

What do you get if you cross the Atlantic with the *Titanic*?

Halfway.

How did the captain of the *Titanic* know when his ship was going down?

Well, he had a sinking feeling.

What do you call a breakfast sandwich with mussels?

The Arnold Shellfish 'n' egger.

What do you get when you cross a kangaroo with a puppet who lives in a garbage can?

Oscar the Pouch.

What do you call a super pig who can climb up the side of buildings?

Spiderham.

Would Little Miss Muffet share her curds?

No whey.

Don't diss me like this, Muffy-baby!

What would you get if you crossed a great hockey player with a Sea-Doo?

Wayne Jet-Ski.

BEHIND THE PUNCH LINE:
Teaming Up

Comedians often work in teams. One comedian will be the straight man while the other one jokes around. The straight man is the one who sets up the joke, while his or her partner sends back dopey answers or quips. George Burns and Gracie Allen, Laurel and Hardy, Martin and Lewis, and Abbot and Costello are famous for this type of team comedy.

155

What did Huey, Dewey, and Louie say when something was falling on their uncle's head?

"Donald—duck!"

Where did the Arabian knights live?

In sand castles.

What do you get when you cross a serial killer with a pair of jeans?

Jack the Zipper.

Why are the Knights of the Round Table so cheap?

They're always cutting corners.

Quick! To the Blobmobile-or we'll be late for the buffet!

What are the names of the most overweight superheroes?
Fatman and Blobbin.

Who's a lamb's favorite superhero?
B-a-atman.

156

Grumpy, Sleepy, and Dopey were on their lunch break at the diamond mine. Grumpy picked up his lunch box and said, "I really hate peanut butter and liverwurst sandwiches. If I have to eat one more peanut butter and liverwurst sandwich, I'm going to run screaming into the woods." And Sleepy said, "I know what you mean. Every day I open my lunch box and it's the same old thing: salami and catsup. I'm so tired of salami and catsup sandwiches. If I have one again today, I'm going to go jump in the river." And Dopey said, "Gee, I have a broccoli and mustard sandwich every day. If that's what's in my lunch today, I'll run straight up that hill and stay there." So all three dwarfs carefully opened their lunch boxes and discovered the same thing they ate every day. Grumpy flipped out and ran screaming into the woods, Sleepy jumped in the river, and Dopey ran off up the hill. That evening, the other four dwarfs told Snow White what had happened at lunchtime. "Grumpy and Sleepy always whine about the lunches I make for them, but I don't understand what got into Dopey," said a puzzled Snow White. "He makes his own lunch!" ✩

What's green and sings?

Elvis Parsley.

What do you get when you put Worf in a dryer?

Static Klingon.

Why couldn't the Tin Man join in the card game?

They were playing Hearts.

What did Dorothy do when her dog got stuck?

She called a Toto truck.

Why was Cinderella thrown off the baseball team?

She kept running away from the ball.

157

What do you get when you cross Cinderella with a barber?

Glass clippers.

What do you get when you cross Cinderella with a rabbit?

A hare ball.

What do you call a famous pirate who always skips school?

Captain Hooky.

What did the chicken say to Arnold Schwarzenegger?

"I'll be bock . . . bock, bock."

I'll be bock... bock, bock.

What barbarian king ate up the Roman Empire?

Attila the Hungry.

What Greek king was purple and conquered the ancient world?

Alexander the Grape.

Who's young and perky and attacks sports officials?

Buffy the Umpire Slayer.

Who was the worst-tempered composer ever?

Ludwig van Beastoven.

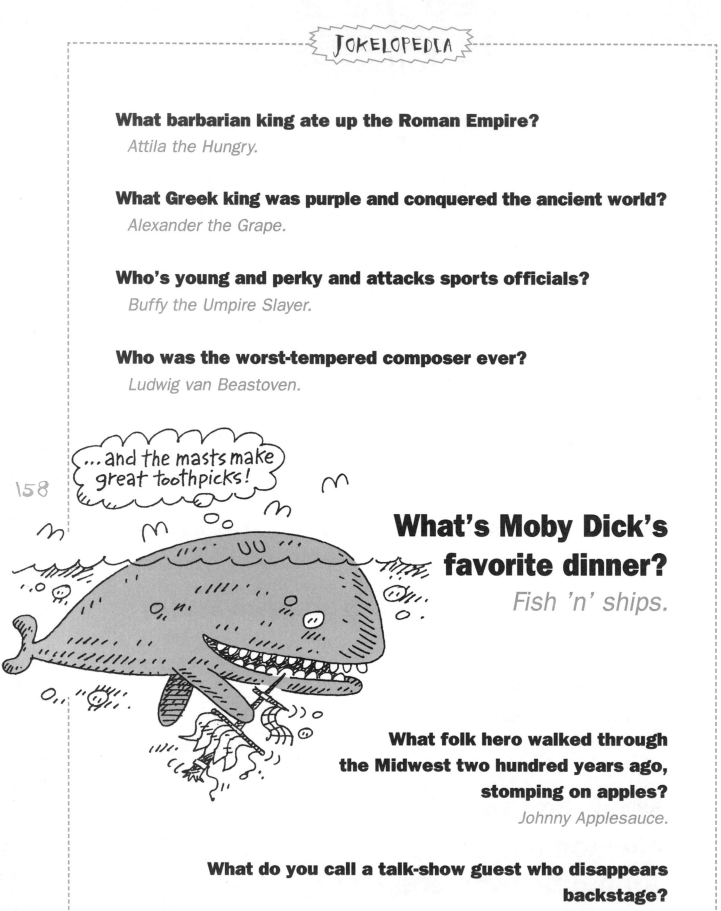

...and the masts make great toothpicks!

158

What's Moby Dick's favorite dinner?

Fish 'n' ships.

What folk hero walked through the Midwest two hundred years ago, stomping on apples?

Johnny Applesauce.

What do you call a talk-show guest who disappears backstage?

The Phantom of the Oprah.

The Three Stooges

The Three Stooges were the ultimate slapstick comedians. Just picture three big men trying to fit through a tiny door all at once, and you'll have a good mental image of the Stooges. The Howard brothers, Moses (Moe), Jerome (Curly), and Shemp, were the original Stooges. They performed in vaudeville shows during the 1920s and 1930s before becoming movie stars. Larry Fine replaced Shemp in 1935. Actor Ted Healy, who played their straight man in films for many years, explained the concept behind the name. "A stooge is a guess-man. You can never guess what he's going to do next." The Three Stooges were great because they were so unpredictable. Even their classic poke-in-the-eye, slap-in-the-face, punch-in-the-belly routine had funny variations and consequences.

THE STOOGES GO SLEUTHING FOR GIGGLES AND HOWLS!

THE THREE STOOGES
SHEMP · LARRY · MOE

WHO DONE IT?

with
CHRISTINE McINTYRE · RALPH DUNN
CHARLES KNIGHT · EMIL SITKA
DUKE YORK · DUDLEY DICKERSON
Directed by EDWARD BER
Produced by HUGH McC

What's black and white and black and
white?

101 Dalmatians.

Goldilocks was walking along one sunny afternoon when she found a beautiful house in the woods. The door was open, so she walked right in. There she found a table set with three bowls of steaming porridge. "Hello?" she called out, but no one was home. She tried the first bowl, but it was too hot. She tried the second bowl, but it was too cold. Then she tried the third bowl, and it was just right. "Wow," she said, once she had finished the meal. "Now I'm feeling very sleepy." So she wandered around looking for a bed. She couldn't find one anywhere on the bottom floor. Finally, she found a staircase at one end of the house. She climbed up the steps and went into the first room. There was a great big bed in the middle of the room, so Goldilocks jumped right in. "Yikes!" she exclaimed. "This one's too hard!" She wandered into the next room. There she found another bed, and hopped right in it. But it was too soft. By this time, Goldilocks was very tired. She went into the third room, and yelled out in surprise. There were three pink pigs cowering in the corner of the room. "Wait a second," she said. "You guys are in the wrong fairy tale."

"No, we're not," answered one of the pigs. "Don't you know this is a two-story house?"

161

What do Tarzan and Jane sing at Christmastime?

Jungle Bells.

Yes...feel the Force, young Skywhopper! Now, ketchup you will need...

What do you get when you cross Darth Vader's son with a hamburger?

The Luke Skywhopper.

Silly Silly Song

(sing to your own tune)

162

Goosy Lucy
does the watusi
To Michael Jackson
And sometimes Debussy.

(She also does
an okey-dokey
Hoky-Pokey.)

SOUNDING A FUNNY NOTE

Bust a Gut in the Band Room

What kind of music do they play at Stonehenge?

Hard rock.

What kind of music do they play at a playground?

Swing.

What kind of music do they play at a soft-drink factory?

Pop.

What kind of music do they play at a construction site?

Heavy metal.

How many country musicians does it take to change a lightbulb?

Five: One to change the bulb, and four to sing about how much they'll miss the old one.

How many folk musicians does it take to change a lightbulb?

Forty: One to change the bulb, and thirty-nine to complain that it's electric.

What happens when you drop a piano down a mine?

A minor B-flat.

What do you get when you drop a piano on an army base?

A major B-flat.

Why didn't the opera singer get a job on the cruise ship?

Because she was afraid of the high Cs.

What is a musician's favorite cereal?

Flute Loops.

When is a tire a bad singer?

When it's flat.

Uh-Oh....

Click!

PRACTICAL JOKES

Beginner Version

Use Krazy Glue to attach a quarter to the sidewalk. Watch people try to pick it up. Warning: don't try this on a busy sidewalk or street.

Advanced Version

Attach a dollar to a long piece of fishing line. Pull it along a sidewalk and watch people try to grab it. If someone comes close, jerk the fishing line and pull it out of his or her reach while you hide.

165

The conductor of a symphony orchestra was having a lot of trouble with one of the percussionists. The conductor talked and talked and talked with him, but his performance just didn't improve. Finally, in front of the whole orchestra, the conductor said, "When a musician just can't play his instrument well and doesn't get better when he is given help, they take away the instrument, give him two sticks, and make him a drummer." A voice from the percussion section replied: "And if he can't play even that, they take away one of his sticks and make him a conductor." ☆

Last night my school orchestra played Beethoven.

Beethoven lost.

What's the difference between an onion and a banjo?

I wouldn't cry if you chopped up the banjo!

Why is Homer Simpson bad at singing scales?

He always gets stuck at "Doh!"

Why did the band eat rabbit stew for a whole week?

They wanted to play hip-hop.

What did the drummer say when his band teacher told him he had no rhythm?

"That's because I'm beat."

I'm sure it's just temporary...

166

How do you catch a percussionist who's on the run?

Use a snare drum.

Why did the boy stop practicing the violin at Christmas?

Because his mother asked for peace on earth.

What's the world's second-oldest rock group?

The Rolling Flintstones.

Why did the Beatles break up?

They started to bug each other.

The Simpsons

Who would guess that a family of five yellow, bug-eyed, four-fingered people with bad overbites and weird hairdos would ever see the light of day on television—much less keep a show going for over ten years?

Guess again. The Simpson family—parents Homer and Marge and kids Bart, Lisa, and Maggie—are the stars of *The Simpsons,* a cartoon show that has far exceeded all expectations. Created by a cartoonist named Matt Groening, the show is both wickedly funny and very intelligent, appealing to kids and adults alike. Groening has said that keeping the jokes fresh is one of the biggest challenges to keeping a show like *The Simpsons* alive for so long, so he makes sure to always insert what he calls "freeze-frame gags," which are jokes that require you to tape the show and then watch it again in freeze-frame motion in order to catch them. Funny guest stars who lend their distinctive voices to the show are another way to keep it fresh. Good writing is the secret to good comedy, and *The Simpsons* is no exception. A crack team of writers ensures that viewers will keep coming back to watch Bart write new messages on his chalkboard. Quirkiness and an ability to keep the jokes coming—two signs of greatness in comic television.

Two boys were camping in the backyard. Late at night they started wondering what time it was. "Start singing really loudly," one of them suggested.

"How will that help?" asked the other boy.

"Just do it," insisted the first.

They both started singing as loudly as they could. Moments later, a neighbor threw open her window and shouted, "Keep it down! Don't you know it's three o'clock in the morning?" ✩

What do you get when you cross an orchestra with a bunch of monkeys?
A chimp-phony.

168

Why did the trombone player get kicked out of the band?
Because he kept letting things slide.

Why can't you sleep during band practice?
Because it's too noisy, silly.

What happened to the house built of cymbals?
The whole thing came crashing down.

When is a tuba good for your teeth?
When it's a tuba toothpaste.

THE MAKING OF A COMEDIAN

Step 5: Sequencing and the "Play Frame"

Telling a joke can produce a chuckle, but tell two or three jokes in the proper sequence and you can have your audience rolling on the floor. The classic joke sequence is the "Why did the chicken cross the road?" series, where the punch line or question varies slightly with each telling. This method works really well for two reasons: first, your listener is already warmed up, and wants to keep laughing; second, you're playing off an expectation. The audience expects to hear the classic joke, but instead gets a new, alternate joke. This makes the joke twice as funny. It's like a clown hitting someone in the face with a pie, and then his victim asking for ice cream on the side.

When you've been telling jokes and your giddy friends are laughing, it's easy to keep them going; in psychology, this state is referred to as a "play frame." A play frame is a situation that makes people expect everything to be funny. For instance, if you're watching a sitcom like *Friends,* or reading a joke book, you expect funny things! You're more prepared to laugh than when you're watching the news. This is one reason why "Top Ten" lists work so well: the list is a series of ten jokes, and you're looking forward to laughing at all of them.

169

Why did the mandolin go the psychiatrist?

It was tired of being high-strung.

What did the grouchy trumpet say to the trumpeteer?

Why did the sheet music run away from the singer?

She kept hitting all the notes.

What do you get when you cross a sink with a bugle?

Taps.

What do you get when a rhinoceros steps on your record?

A smashed hit.

176

Don't give me any of your lip!

♪ That love look in your eyes... as you slurp down those flies... ♪ it's witchcraft... ♪

Can you can a piano?

No, but you can tuna fish.

How do you make a bandstand?

Take away their chairs.

Why couldn't the concertgoer get her money back when the singer was off-key?

Because she paid the flat rate.

A mangy-looking guy goes into a diner and orders a cup of coffee. The waitress says, "No way. I don't think you can pay for it."

The guy says, "You're right. I don't have any money, but if I show you something you haven't seen before, will you give me a cup?"

The waitress says, "Only if what you show me isn't gross."

"Deal!" says the guy, and he reaches into his coat pocket and pulls out a hamster. He puts the hamster on the counter and it runs across the room and up the piano in the corner, jumps on the keyboard, and starts playing. And the hamster is really good.

The waitress says, "You're right. I've never seen anything like that before. That hamster is truly good on the piano." The guy drinks the coffee and asks for another.

"Money or another miracle, or else no coffee," says the waitress.

The guy reaches into his coat again and pulls out a frog. He puts the frog on the counter, and the frog starts to sing. He has a marvelous voice and great pitch. He's a fine singer. A stranger from the other end of the counter rushes over to the guy and offers him $300 for the frog. The guy says, "It's a deal." He takes the money and gives the frog to the stranger.

The stranger runs out of the diner.

The waitress says to the guy, "Are you some kind of nut? You sold a singing frog for $300? It must be worth millions. You must be crazy."

"Not so," says the guy. "The hamster is also a ventriloquist." ☆

Why did the drummer bring a chicken to band practice?

He needed new drumsticks.

This... ...solo... ...is... ...killing... ...me...

What do you call a keyboard with good manners?

An upright piano.

What kind of music do long-distance truckers listen to?

Cross-country music.

172

ha-ha!

ha-ha!

ha-ha!

ATHLETIC ANTICS

Really Sock It to 'Em in the Gym

What's a good place to take your golf clubs after the game?

To a tee party.

Why do pro baseball players spin around a lot?

To get ready for the whirl series.

What's the best thing to drink during a marathon?

Running water.

Are baseball umpires good eaters?

Yes—they always clean their plates.

What job did Dracula Junior have at the baseball stadium?

He was the bat boy for night games.

How can you tell the difference between a judge and a skating rink?

One brings people to justice; the other brings people to just ice.

What position does a pig play in football?

Swinebacker.

174

SALESMAN: Try this new bandage. You can swim, water-ski, snorkel, or scuba dive with it on!
INJURED CUSTOMER: That's great! I couldn't do any of those things before I hurt myself!

LITTLE LEAGUE COACH: What would you do if it were the bottom of the ninth with two outs and three runners on base?
RELIEF PITCHER: Come out of the dugout so I could see the action better!

BOY: Coach, why does that guy look so mad when he runs a marathon?
COACH: He's a cross-country runner.

Why did the rubber band go to the baseball game?

It wanted to enjoy the seventh-inning stretch.

Why don't eggs make good quarterbacks?

When their defense cracks, they're too quick to scramble.

Why do basketball players stay home during the off-season?

They aren't allowed to travel.

What do you get when you cross a basketball team with cinnamon crullers?

Dunkin' donuts.

How is a basketball player like a baby?

They both dribble!

What has four wheels and grows on a vine?

A skategourd.

Why do scientists love baseball?

They love looking at slides.

Where do baseball pitchers learn new pitches?

They look in the en-strike-lopedia.

When do ballplayers get emotional?

When they choke up on the bat.

Helpful Hint

To help you speed up your morning routine, try the following time-saving tips. Smear food on your face before bed. When you wake up, lick it off—better than a breakfast bar!

Keep your clothes in the car and get dressed on the way to school.

Shower? Who needs it? Just ask your parents to drive through a car wash with the windows down. But be warned—that big whirling brush really tickles!

175

Why did the baseball player take his bat to the library?

His teacher told him to hit the books.

What's black and white and never right?

A hockey referee.

What kind of player gives refunds?

A quarterback!

Also, the spinning makes me nauseous...

176

Why did the athlete take up bowling?

He thought it would be up his alley.

oe was late meeting Sarah at the corner, and his shorts and T-shirt were all wet. He said he had been playing in the sprinkler but couldn't dry his clothes.

"Why not?" asked Sarah.

"Because I couldn't fit in the dryer." ☆

Why couldn't anyone find the deck of cards?

They got lost in the shuffle.

What game do tornadoes like to play?

Twister.

SPOTLIGHT

Margaret Cho

Margaret Cho has faced many obstacles on her way to success. The San Francisco–raised Korean-American comedian (who is, coincidentally, the daughter of a joke-book author!) wrote and starred in her own cable-TV comedy special in 1994, *HBO Comedy Half-Hour: Margaret Cho,* for which she won an American Comedy Award. Cho was then offered the opportunity to star in her own network TV show, *All-American Girl,* on ABC. The show was about the comic culture clashes faced by an American girl with Asian immigrant parents. But it was later canceled and Cho found herself without a job.

After touring comedy clubs nationwide, Cho wrote and produced a one-woman Broadway show in 1999. In it she described the process of losing and regaining her Asian-American identity in Hollywood. Cho has made a name for herself by accentuating her Korean heritage and contrasting it to the typical American experience. Her Broadway show seemed to be her way of saying that celebrating our own individuality is an important step in gaining the acceptance of those around us.

CALENDAR CUTUPS

It's that time of the year again:
Will February March?
No, but April May.

If April showers bring May flowers,
what do May flowers bring?
Pilgrims.

What do you get when you cross a soccer player with a cow?
The team Jersey.

What's the difference between a soccer player and a dog?
The soccer player wears a team uniform, the dog just pants.

Why don't matches play baseball?
One strike and they're out.

What do baseball players give their fiancées?
Diamonds.

What do you get when you cross a baseball pitcher with a carpet?
A throw rug.

What do you get when you cross a baseball player with a monster?
A double-header.

Why is it a good idea to have a frog on your baseball team?
They're good at catching pop flies.

Thath the lath thime I thry to cath one with my thongue...

178

Why did the pitcher bring an old pocket watch to his games?

So he could wind up before throwing the ball.

Where do hair colorists sit when they go to baseball games?

In the bleachers.

Why did the batter tear off his clothes after he hit a home run?

He wanted his team to have a winning streak.

Do old bikers ever die?

No, they just get recycled.

Why did the unicycle?

Well, she wasn't about to walk!

There goes Another homer! "Curve ball" you said—"He can't hit the curve" you said...

Well, if you'd let me pitch for a change, I'd show you a proper curve ball...

179

Why did the golfer bring two pairs of socks to the tournament?

In case she got a hole in one.

What do you get when you cross a golfer with a library?

Book clubs.

Let's GO, featherweight!

Who's a better boxer, a bean or a chicken?
The bean—he's no chicken.

Why was the prizefighter fired from his job?
He was always punching out early.

What do you get when you cross a golf club with a Chevy?
A backseat driver.

Why are a golfer's pants never wrinkled?
Because golfers use nine-irons.

How did the trampolinist beat the prizefighter?
Every time he was knocked down, he bounced right back.

Why did the fight fans keep getting punched?
Because they were sitting in the box seats!

Why does it take longer to run from second base to third base than it does from first to second?
Because there's a shortstop between second and third.

How do gymnasts feel after a routine?
Head over heels.

BEHIND THE PUNCH LINE:
One-Person Shows

A one-person show is, as its name suggests, a comedy show performed by only one actor. Such shows are usually done either as a monologue or as a series of skits. A monologue is a long comic piece that is spoken without breaks. Skits are shorter pieces, performed with breaks in between. An actor skilled at impersonation or who wishes to portray several different characters as part of her show will often use skits. Actors looking for a more dramatic presentation will go for the monologue.

One-person shows are difficult because the focus is all on one actor, who often is the writer, director, and producer of the show as well. But for an actor who wants to focus on one topic that means a lot to her—for example, race or ethnic heritage, or a particular problem she has overcome in her life—it can be a good way to express herself.

181

What game does Godzilla like best?

Squash.

What's a Chrysler's favorite game?

Dodge ball.

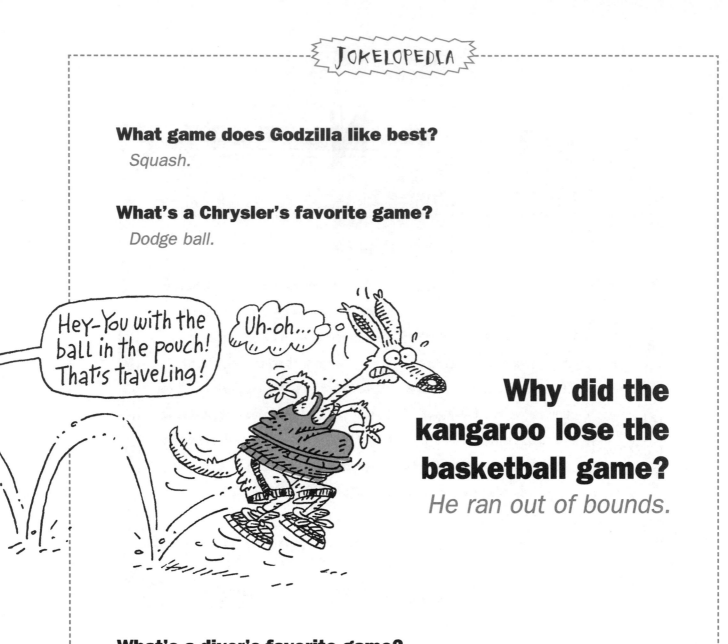

Hey–You with the ball in the pouch! That's traveling!

Uh-oh....

Why did the kangaroo lose the basketball game?

He ran out of bounds.

What's a diver's favorite game?

Pool.

What kind of match doesn't light on fire?

A tennis match.

How come the football player didn't score a touchdown?

His flight was stuck in a holding pattern.

Why was the football player following the other team's linebacker?

Because the grass is always greener on the other side of defense.

FUNNY BUSINESS

Humor at Work

Why did the Tiger eat the tightrope walker?

How many carpenters does it take to screw in a lightbulb?

Hey! That's the electrician's job!

How many jugglers does it take to screw in a lightbulb?

One, but he uses at least three bulbs.

He wanted a well-balanced meal.

Where do butchers dance?

At the meat ball.

What's a gambler's favorite game show?

The Dice is Right.

How do garbagemen break up with their girlfriends?

They just dump 'em.

A local business was looking for office help. The owners put a sign in the window that read: "HELP WANTED. Must be able to type, must be good with a computer, and must be bilingual. We are an Equal Opportunity Employer." A short time later, a dog trotted up to the window, saw the sign, and went inside. He looked at the receptionist and wagged his tail, then walked over to the sign, looked at it, and whined. The receptionist got the idea and told the office manager. The office manager looked at the dog and was surprised, to say the least. However, the dog looked determined, so the manager led him into his office. Inside, the dog jumped up on a chair and stared at the manager. The manager said, "I can't hire you. The sign says you have to be able to type." The dog jumped down, went to the typewriter, and typed out a perfect letter. He took out the page and trotted over to the manager and gave it to him, then jumped back on the chair. The manager was stunned, but then told the dog, "The sign says you have to be good with a computer." The dog went to the computer and entered a program that ran perfectly the first time. By now, the manager was totally dumbfounded! He looked at the dog and said, "I realize that you are a very intelligent dog and have some interesting skills. However, I *still* can't give you the job." The dog jumped down, went to a copy of the sign, and put his paw on the sentence that read "We are an Equal Opportunity Employer." The manager said, "Yes, but the sign *also* says that you must speak two languages." The dog looked calmly at the manager and said, "Meow." ☆

184

ACME
KITTY TOYS,
INC.

Meow...
meow, meow...
mee-oow!
purrr...
meow..meow...

PRACTICAL JOKE

How to freak out people in a crowded elevator:

- Make explosion noises whenever someone hits a button.
- Stand silently in a corner, facing the wall. There is scientific proof that if you do this long enough, the other passengers will all turn and face the wall, too.
- Meow occasionally.
- Bet the other passengers that you can fit a quarter in your nose.
- Yell "Ding!" at each floor.

185

Who gets the most respect in the circus?

The tall man—everyone looks up to him.

Did you hear that the fire-eater got engaged?

He ran into an old flame.

Did you hear how hard it is to get a job as a sword-swallower?

There's cutthroat competition.

A man who had been working for the circus for many years as Mr. Tiny, the shortest man alive, agreed to meet with a local newspaper reporter one Sunday to be interviewed. The reporter arrived on time but was surprised to be greeted by a man who was nearly six feet tall. The reporter thought he must be in the wrong place and asked for Mr. Tiny.

"That's me," said the man.

"But you're supposed to be short!" said the reporter.

Mr. Tiny said, "I told you—this is my day off." ☆

Why did the pantyhose need a lawyer?
They were on the run.

Why did the brownie mix need a lawyer?
It was battered.

ha-ha!

Why did the sticker need a lawyer?
It was ripped off.

What are a gas station attendant's favorite shoes?
Pumps.

What are a plumber's favorite shoes?
Clogs.

If athletes get athlete's foot, then what do astronauts get?
Missile toe.

Ben Stiller

Ben Stiller has comedy in his blood—he is the son of two famous comedians, husband and wife comedy team Jerry Stiller and Anne Meara. Stiller grew up in Hollywood, shooting home movies with a Super 8 camera when not producing plays with his sister Amy. Ben began his showbiz career as a comedian, and has also made a name for himself in Hollywood as an actor, writer, producer, and director. His biggest role as an actor was probably that of Ted, the poor guy who just wanted to find love with his old sweetheart Mary in the film *There's Something About Mary.* Before that, however, young Stiller wrote and produced his own sketch-comedy television show, *The Ben Stiller Show,* for MTV. Although the show was canceled, it launched his career and won him several awards. He later wrote, produced, directed, and starred in the film *Reality Bites.*

Stiller's comic genius lies in his ability to create very realistic characters who find themselves in very funny situations. Despite his success in comedy, Stiller says, "I've never really felt like a funny, funny guy. I've never been Mr. Life of the Party." Clearly, juggling five professions makes you very humble!

A frog went to a bank to apply for a loan. Patty Stack, the woman in charge of loans, asked if he had anything to leave for collateral. "Don't worry," she said. "When you pay back the loan, we'll return it to you." He showed her a small porcelain statue and said, "This is what I have. It is a family heirloom and it's very special to me."

She took it to the bank president and said, "There's a frog out there who wants a loan, and this is what he gave me as proof that we can trust him, but I don't know what it is. Should I give him the money?"

The bank president said, "Why, that's a knickknack, Patty Stack, give that frog a loan." ✩

188

What do you call a king's sore throat?

A royal pain in the neck.

Did you hear about the wizard who became a film director?

He really made movie magic.

How does the snake charmer sign his letters?

"Love and hisses."

Where do spies do their shopping?

At the snooper market.

Why did the fisherman go deaf?

He had problems with his herring.

What's the Man of Steel's household chore?

Supper, man.

A young man at a construction site always bragged that he was stronger than everyone else there. He would especially make fun of one of the older workmen. After a while, the older man had had enough. "Why don't you put your money where your mouth is?" he said. "I'll bet a week's pay that I can haul something in a wheelbarrow over to that building that you won't be able to wheel back."

"You're on," the braggart replied. "Let's see what you got."

The old man reached out and grabbed the wheelbarrow by the handles. Then, nodding to the young man, he said with a smile, "All right. Get in." ☆

Mortimer the Magnificent tried for ages to get into the circus. When Trevor's Traveling Carnival came to town, he begged and pleaded with the owner to watch his act. The owner finally agreed. Mortimer stepped into the center ring and began flapping his arms wildly, and within moments he rose off the ground. As he started going higher and faster, he began to do all kinds of tricks: barrel rolls and loop-the-loops, swan dives and somersaults. After about 20 minutes of this, Mortimer floated back down to the ground and landed gracefully right in front of the circus owner. The owner took a puff on his cigar and asked, "So. What else do you do besides bird impersonations?" ☆

Hmm...I wonder if I can pay him in birdseed?

A private eye had just moved into his new office when there was a knock at the door. He wanted to make a good impression, so he yelled "Come in!" and picked up the phone, pretending to be talking to someone important. The visitor waited patiently, and after a minute the detective hung up the phone and said, "As you can see, I'm very busy. What can I do for you?"

"Not much," replied the visitor. "I'm here to hook up your phone."

190

What do you get when you cross a comedian with crochet?

A knit wit.

Why couldn't the bodybuilder cross the road?

The traffic was too heavy.

A woman is sitting in a park one day, watching two men work. The first man digs a hole, then the second man fills it back up with dirt. Then the first man digs another hole, and again, the second man fills it back up. They keep doing this over and over again. Finally, the woman asks them, "Why do you keep digging holes and then filling them back in?" One of the guys replies, "Well, usually there's a third guy here who puts in the tree, but he's out sick today."

Why did the comedian put on his sneakers?

He wanted to tell a running joke.

Why did the young woman take the job at the glue factory?

It was fast paste.

The dentist took one look at Billy's mouth and said, "That's the biggest cavity I've ever seen. That's the biggest cavity I've ever seen."

Billy looked at him and said, "I heard you, Doc. You don't have to repeat yourself."

"I didn't. That was an echo." ☆

191

Why did the upholsterer quit her job?

She was worn out.

Three boys were watching a fire truck roaring down the street with a beautiful Dalmatian riding on top of it.

The first boy said, "They use him to pull children to safety."

"You're wrong," said the second boy. "He helps keep people away from the fire."

"Both of you are wrong," announced the third. "They use him to find the fire hydrant." ☆

192

BEHIND THE PUNCH LINE:
Homonyms

You may be thinking, "Oh no! Not a grammar lesson! Isn't this book supposed to be *funny*?"

However, if you want to be a comedian, it helps to know your language inside and out. After all, wordplay is a big part of telling jokes.

The English language is full of crazy words that sound exactly the same but aren't spelled alike and have completely different meanings.

These are called *homonyms*.

An example of a joke that makes good use of a homonym:

Q: What's the difference between a bus driver and a bad cold?

A: One knows the stops and the other one stops the nose!

The joke is funny because "knows" and "nose" sound the same but mean very different things. Telling a joke like this makes you look very, very smart!

What happened when the dry cleaner was mugged?

He pressed charges.

A young woman is speeding down a freeway when she is stopped by a highway patrol officer. The officer asks if he could please see her driver's license. The woman replies angrily, "I wish you guys would make up your mind. Just yesterday you take away my license, and now you expect me to show it to you!"

Two 90-year-old men, Moe and Sam, have been friends all their lives. Sam is dying, so Moe comes to visit him. "Sam," says Moe, "you know how we both loved baseball all our lives. Sam, you have to do me one favor. When you go, somehow you've got to tell me if there's baseball in heaven."

Sam looks up at Moe from his deathbed and says, "Moe, you've been my friend for many years. I'll do that for you." And with that, he passes on.

It is midnight a couple of nights later. Moe is sound asleep when a distant voice calls out to him, "Moe. . . . Moe. . . ."

"Who is it?" says Moe, sitting up suddenly. "Who is it?"

"Moe, it's Sam."

"Come on. You're not Sam. Sam died."

"I'm telling you," insists the voice. "It's me, Sam!"

"Sam? Is that you? Where are you?"

"I'm in heaven," says Sam, "and I've got to tell you, I've got some good news and some bad news."

"Tell me the good news first," says Moe.

"The good news," says Sam, "is that there is baseball in heaven."

"Really?" says Moe. "That's wonderful! What's the bad news?"

"You're pitching Tuesday!"

WHOA! Pop flies are a cinch up here!

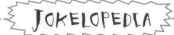

Why are cowboys bad at math?

They're always rounding things up.

Why didn't the cashier get the punch line?

It didn't register.

Why did the boy quit his job at the eraser factory?

His work rubbed him the wrong way.

A woman frantically calls the fire department to report a fire in her neighborhood.

The dispatcher asks, "How do we get there?"

The woman replies, "Don't you still have those little red fire trucks?"

Why did the baker sell his bread only to the rich and famous?

He wanted to work for the upper crust.

What did the baker think of the joke?

He got a rise out of it.

Why did everyone find the baker funny?

He had a rye sense of humor.

How did the baker get so wealthy?

He made a lot of dough.

An astronaut graduated near the bottom of his class. On his first mission into space, he was teamed up with a monkey. They each got an envelope that they were to open once they got into orbit, with instructions for their mission. Once they had blasted off and were in space, the monkey opened his envelope, read the instructions, and began flicking buttons and hitting switches. The astronaut opened up his own envelope and found a note that read:

"Feed the monkey." ✩

Hey-there're bananas in the hold if you want one!

How does the vaudeville player save so much money?

He gets everything for a song and a dance.

Why did the engineer leave locomotive school?

She felt she already had enough training.

Why couldn't the sailors play cards?

Because they were standing on the deck!

Why did the human cannonball choose this line of work?

He wanted to be a big shot.

A man goes ice fishing. He takes out an ice pick and begins to hack away. He hears a loud voice from above saying, "There're no fish there." He goes to another spot and starts to pick away. Again comes the voice: "There're no fish there either." He tries a third spot. Once more, he hears the voice from above say, "Nope. Not there either." Finally, the man, growing a little nervous, looks up and asks, "Are you God?" The response from above booms, "No. I'm the arena manager." ☆

What do angels say when they answer the telephone?

"Halo!"

What do you get when you cross a secretary with a CD player?

A stereotype.

Why did the journalist go to the ice-cream parlor?

She wanted to get the scoop.

Why did the coffee shop waitress love her job?

Because there were so many perks.

What did the farmer say when he fell in the haystack?

"Somebody bale me out!"

What did the tailor say after his client fired him?

"Suit yourself."

A fire started on some grasslands near a farm. The county fire department was called to put out the fire, but it was more than they could handle. Someone suggested calling in the nearby volunteer firefighting crew. Nobody knew if the volunteers would be of any help, but they called them anyway.

The volunteers arrived in a beat-up old fire truck. They rumbled straight toward the fire, drove right into the middle of the flames, and stopped! The volunteer firemen jumped off the truck and started frantically spraying water in all directions. Soon they had snuffed out the center of the fire, breaking the blaze into two smaller parts that they then easily put out.

I can smell the brakes overheating...

197

Watching all this, the farmer was so impressed with the volunteer fire department's work and was so grateful that his farm had been spared that right there on the spot he presented the volunteers with a check for $1,000. A local news reporter asked the volunteer fire captain what the department planned to do with the funds.

"That should be obvious," he replied, wiping ashes off his coat. "The first thing we're going to do is get the brakes fixed on our fire truck!"

Why did the tailor go to the farm?

So he could sew some oats.

What do farmers plant in their sofas?

Couch potatoes.

When are farmers mean?

When they pull the ears off corn!

O ne day, a circus arrived in the small town of Biggy-Wiggy. They set up a tent so big that all the Biggy-Wiggians could fit underneath it. The tent was red with blue stripes and had a large flag at its peak. The Biggy-Wiggians could see the red-and-blue-striped tent and its large flag no matter where they stood in Biggy-Wiggy. The little Biggy-Wiggians all wanted the bigger Biggy-Wiggians to take them to the circus, so there was a lot of Biggy-Wiggy begging. All the Biggy-Wiggy girls and all the Biggy-Wiggy boys bought tickets to the show.

The Biggy-Wiggy circus had more animals than even the biggest Biggy-Wiggian could shake a stick at. There were thirty Biggy-Wiggy elephants with sixty Biggy-Wiggy tusks, forty Biggy-Wiggy leopards all with Biggy-Wiggy spots, ten Biggy-Wiggy dancing bears, five Biggy-Wiggy seals in five Biggy-Wiggy tanks, and ninety Biggy-Wiggy lions with ninety of the most ferocious Biggy-Wiggy roars. There were Biggy-Wiggy piggies dressed in Biggy-Wiggy frills and Biggy-Wiggy performing dogs all with Biggy-Wiggy wags.

There were clowns stuffed into Biggy-Wiggy buggies. There were even Biggy-Wiggy belly dancers with Biggy-wiggy wiggles.

The first night of the circus, all the Biggy-Wiggians with their Biggy-Wiggy tickets filed into the red-and-blue-striped tent with its large flag. They sat in Biggy-Wiggy bleachers and bought Biggy-Wiggy popcorn and Biggy-Wiggy pop. They stared down at the three biggest Biggy-Wiggy circus rings ever. The show was about to begin and all the Biggy-Wiggians held their Biggy-Wiggy breaths. A single clown came out and stood in the middle of the middle ring.

"What's two plus two plus two minus four?" the Biggy Wiggy clown asked.

A Biggy-Wiggy hush fell across the Biggy-Wiggy crowd. None of them were very good at math.

"I'm sorry folks, but this Biggy-Wiggy show can't go on," said the Biggy-Wiggy clown, and left.

Why didn't the clown continue?

There were three rings but no one answered. ✰

Why did the stagehand quit her job?

She wanted a change of scenery.

A sailor met a pirate, and they started to talk about their adventures at sea. The sailor noticed that the pirate had a peg leg, a hook, and an eye patch. The sailor asked, "So, how did you end up with the peg leg?"

The pirate replied, "We were in a storm at sea, and I was swept overboard into a school of sharks. Just as my men were pulling me out, a shark bit my leg off."

"Wow!" exclaimed the sailor. "How did you get that hook?"

"Well," replied the pirate, "we boarded an enemy ship and were battling the other sailors with swords. One of them cut off my hand."

"Incredible!" remarked the sailor. "How did you get the eye patch?"

"A seagull dropping fell into my eye," replied the pirate.

"You lost your eye to a seagull dropping?" the sailor asked in surprise.

"Well," said the pirate, "it was my first day with the hook."

200

What kind of trains do ballerinas take?

Tutu trains.

What did the fisherman say to the magician?

"Pick a cod, any cod."

A cowboy went to a motel on Friday, stayed for two days, and left on Friday. How was that possible?

His horse was named Friday.

Why are perfume salespeople so smart?

They have good scents.

A woman was having lunch with her two friends and asked them where she could buy windows. The first friend, who loved building things, said, "Try a hardware store."

The second friend said, "What are you talking about? Try a software store!" ☆

What did the milkmaid say to the anxious butter?

"You'll have to wait your churn."

Does a roller coaster like its work?

It has its ups and downs.

The groundskeeper at a park heard a commotion in the lake. He saw a man thrashing around in the water, and said to him, "Hey, don't you know there's no swimming allowed here?"

"I'm drowning!" screamed the man, trying to keep his head above water.

"Oh well, I guess that's allowed," said the groundskeeper. ☆

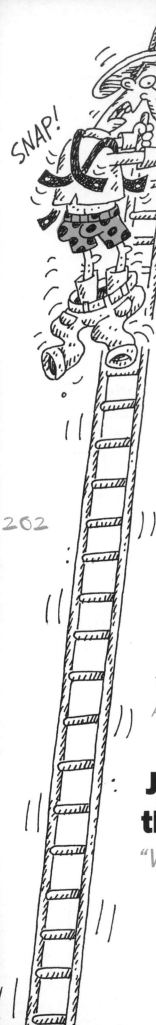

SNAP!

202

How do you learn to be a judge?

Mostly through trial and error.

Why was the fireman lovesick?

He couldn't get over an old flame.

Why do firemen slide down a pole in the firehouse?

Because it's too hard to slide up.

Why do firemen wear red suspenders?

To keep their pants up.

What did the owner of the coffee shop give to her new employees?

A list of do's and donuts.

What has four wheels and flies?

A garbage truck!

Julio's sister asked him what he thought about his job at the plant.

"Well, it's growing on me," said Julio.

DOC-DOC JOKES

You Need a Lot of Patients For This Chapter!

NURSE: Doctor, there is an invisible man in the waiting room.
DOCTOR: Tell hlm I can't see him.

PATIENT: Doctor, I need help. I can never remember what I just said.
DOCTOR: When did you first notice this problem?
PATIENT: Notice what problem?

PATIENT: If the doctor can't see me now, I'm leaving.
NURSE: Calm down. What's wrong with you?
PATIENT: I have a serious wait problem.

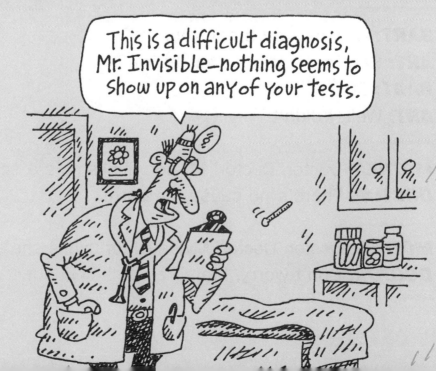

This is a difficult diagnosis, Mr. Invisible—nothing seems to show up on any of your tests.

What two letters of the alphabet spell big trouble for your teeth?

D-K.

What's a Doc-Doc joke?

A knock-knock joke with a cold.

A leopard went to see an eye doctor because he thought he needed a checkup. "What's wrong?" asked the doctor. "Well, doctor," said the leopard, "every time I look at my wife, I see spots before my eyes."

"What's wrong with that?" asked the doctor. "You are a leopard."

"What's that got to do with anything?" asked the leopard. "My wife's a zebra." ✪

204

PATIENT: I'm here for my heart.
DOCTOR: Sorry, I don't have it.

BART: How did you break your leg?
ART: See those steps over there?
BART: Sure.
ART: Well, I didn't!

MOTHER: Doctor, Doctor! My son thinks he's a smoke detector.
DOCTOR: There's no cause for alarm.

MOTHER: Doctor, Doctor! My daughter thinks she's a refrigerator.
DOCTOR: Don't worry, I'm sure she'll chill out.

A man is sitting at home one evening when the doorbell rings. He answers the door to find a six-foot-tall cockroach standing there. The cockroach immediately punches him between the eyes and runs off. The next evening, the man is sitting at home again when the doorbell rings. He answers the door, and the same cockroach is outside. This time, it punches him, kicks him, and karate-chops him before running away. The third evening, the man answers the doorbell to find the same cockroach yet again. It leaps at him and stabs him several times before disappearing. The seriously injured man manages to crawl to the phone and call an ambulance. He is rushed to the hospital and doctors there save his life. The next morning, a doctor asks him what happened. The man explains the attacks by the six-foot-tall cockroach. The doctor thinks for a moment and says, "Yes, I hear there's a nasty bug going around." ✩

205

Why did the clown go to the doctor?

He was feeling a little funny.

When do doctors get angry?

When they run out of patients!

Joe said he wasn't feeling well. "You better call me a doctor," he said to his friend. His friend protested, "But I'd rather call you Joe." ✩

What did one elevator say to the other?

I think I'm coming down with something!

A man went to see his very busy doctor. "Doctor, Doctor!" he said. "I feel like a pack of cards." The doctor replied, "I'll deal with you later." ☆

206

PATIENT: Doctor, Doctor! You've got to help me! Some mornings I wake up and think I'm Donald Duck. Other mornings I think I'm Mickey Mouse.
DOCTOR: Hmm, how long have you been having these Disney spells?

A woman went to her psychiatrist and said, "Doctor, I want to talk to you about my husband. He thinks he's a refrigerator."

"That's not so bad," said the doctor. "It's a rather harmless problem."

"Well, maybe," replied the lady. "But he sleeps with his mouth open and the light keeps me awake." ☆

Dr. Seuss

Theodor Geisel was one of the most famous authors ever. Millions of copies of his 40 books, translated into 20 languages, still fill shelves in bookstores all over the world. Chances are, you can recite a passage from a Theodor Geisel book yourself.

You say you have no idea who we're talking about? That's because Theodor Geisel wrote most of his books under a fake name—Dr. Seuss! He added the "Dr." part because his father always wanted him to become a doctor.

But his real passion was for creating stories and drawing pictures to go with them. Dr. Seuss's silly rhymes and goofy illustrations made his work extremely popular with kids and adults alike. Dr. Seuss wrote his first book after reading an article about how boring kids' books were.

Over the course of his long career, Dr. Seuss wrote and illustrated dozens of books, including *The Cat in the Hat, One Fish Two Fish Red Fish Blue Fish,* and *Horton Hears a Who.* His books are not complicated. Once, a book publisher bet him he could not write a book using only 50 words—and he did: *Green Eggs & Ham.* The publisher never paid him! He could only draw one human face, so all of his characters look alike, but wear different clothes.

One of his most popular books, *How the Grinch Stole Christmas,* was made into a very popular animated movie and, more recently, a feature film starring comedian Jim Carrey.

So even though he didn't become a doctor, we should all be glad that Dr. Seuss found his real calling in life— making people laugh.

A woman called a psychiatrist and said, "Doctor, my brother thinks he's the Easter Bunny."

"How long has this been going on?" asked the doctor.

"A few years," said the woman.

"Goodness, my dear lady! Why didn't you tell anyone sooner?" asked the doctor.

"Because we needed the eggs." ✩

PATIENT: Doctor, Doctor! I keep thinking I'm a $10 bill.
DOCTOR: Go shopping. The change will do you good.

Say "Meow"...

A man went to the psychiatrist and said, "Please help me out, Doc. I think I'm lucky."

The doctor said, "Well, what's wrong with being lucky?"

"Lucky's my cat." ✩

A psychiatrist tells his patient, "I've got good news and bad news. The good news is, you've got a split personality."

"Are you kidding me?" says the patient. "That's the good news? What's the bad?"

The psychiatrist says, "I'm going to have to bill you twice." ✩

A dermatologist says to his patient, "Look, I have a diagnosis for you: you've got Tropical Toe Rash."

The patient says, "Well, I want a second opinion."

"Okay," says the dermatologist. "You're ugly, too." ☆

A man goes to the doctor and says, "I've got a problem, Doc. Sometimes I think I'm a teepee and sometimes I think I'm a wigwam. Teepee, wigwam, wigwam, teepee. I need help!"

"I know what your problem is!" said the doctor. "You're too tents!" ☆

Why did the doctor go to work for the phone company?
He wanted to be an operator.

S even days showed up in the doctor's office.
"What are you doing here?" he asked them.
"Well," they replied, "we're feeling week." ☆

A nurse says to a recovering patient, "You're a very lucky man. The doctor took a gallstone the size of a golf ball out of you."

The patient says, "My goodness. I'd like to thank her. Is she around?"

The nurse says, "No, she thought she'd go golfing." ☆

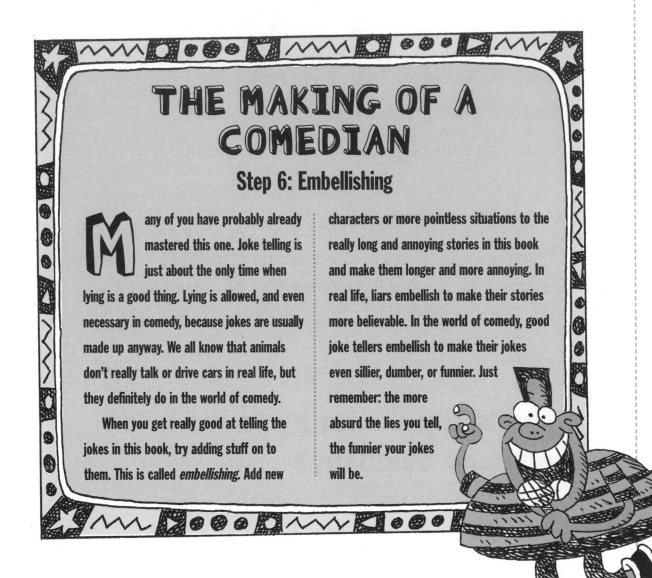

THE MAKING OF A COMEDIAN

Step 6: Embellishing

Many of you have probably already mastered this one. Joke telling is just about the only time when lying is a good thing. Lying is allowed, and even necessary in comedy, because jokes are usually made up anyway. We all know that animals don't really talk or drive cars in real life, but they definitely do in the world of comedy.

When you get really good at telling the jokes in this book, try adding stuff on to them. This is called *embellishing*. Add new characters or more pointless situations to the really long and annoying stories in this book and make them longer and more annoying. In real life, liars embellish to make their stories more believable. In the world of comedy, good joke tellers embellish to make their jokes even sillier, dumber, or funnier. Just remember: the more absurd the lies you tell, the funnier your jokes will be.

A patient went in to see the doctor and the nurse asked her some questions.

"Name?" asked the nurse.

"Sandra Brown," said the patient.

"Address?" asked the nurse.

"106 Main Street."

"Flu?" asked the nurse.

"No, I walked. It's just around the corner."

"I have pimples all over my body!" said the patient to his doctor.

"Is there anything else?" asked the doctor.

The patient says, "No, that zit." ✩

"Doc," said the patient, "my stomach is real bad these days."

"Then send it to bed without supper," said the doctor. ✩

A patient went to the doctor and said, "Doctor, will you give me something for my leg?"

The doctor said, "Well, I don't need it, but I can offer a dollar if you're desperate." ✩

211

A doctor says to his patient, "Well, I've got good news and bad news. The bad news is, you've got a month to live."

"What? That's awful!" says the patient. "What's the good news?"

The doctor says, "I just won the lottery!" ✩

Why did the ham go see a doctor?
It wanted to know if it could be cured.

A patient says to his doctor, "I've thrown my back out again. What should I do?"

The doctor says, "Look through the trash before it's collected!" ✩

A patient goes in to his doctor and says, "Doctor, yesterday I spent all day photographing my nose, and today I can't stop sneezing."

The doctor scratches his chin and asks, "Did you get the pictures back yet?"

"Not yet," says the patient. "Why?"

The doctor says, "Well, obviously, you're developing a cold." ✩

The pediatrician says to Mrs. Jones, "You told me your son had problems eating, but when I examined him, I found he had a broken nose."

Mrs. Jones said, "Well, doctor, you obviously didn't understand what I meant when I said he just pecks at his food." ✩

A terrified mother called 911. "Help me!" she said. "My son just swallowed a fork!"

The 911 operator told her not to worry and that he would send an ambulance over right away.

"What should I do until it arrives?" the mother asked him.

The operator said, "Use a spoon." ✩

"I've swallowed a clock!" yells a patient to his doctor. "Please help me, I feel tick to my stomach." ✩

Hmm... doesn't seem to be Tocks-ic...

TICK TICK TICK TICK..

Why did the doctor keep operating on patients even though he wasn't very good at it?

He needed the practice.

BILL: I went to the eye doctor because I saw fuzzy spots in front of my eyes. The doctor gave me glasses.
BOB: Did the glasses help?
BILL: Yes! I can see the spots much better now!

SURGEON: Nurse, did you put the patient to sleep?
NURSE: Yeah, I just told her some of your jokes.

213

Why did the pie crust go to the dentist?
It needed a filling.

A surgeon steps into the patient's room, looking glum.
"I'm afraid I can't operate," he says.
"Why not?" asks the patient.
"You haven't let me read your operator's manual." ☆

(WARNING: This may be the wurst joke in this book.)

A patient says to his doctor, "I think my throat is wurst."
The doctor says to him, "Ahem—I think you mean 'worse.'"
"No," said the patient. "I mean wurst. Do you know how much it hurts to choke on a sausage?" ☆

A patient says to his doctor, "I think my tonsils need to be taken out."

The doctor says, "I'll make reservations. Would they prefer dinner or dancing?"

A man made an appointment to see a new optometrist. "Doctor," the man says, "I think I'm suffering from poor eyesight."

"Oh, don't worry," said the doctor. "I can just print your bill bigger."

214

"Doctor, I hurt my left hand," said a patient. "Will I be able to play the clarinet?"

"Your hand will heal in a few days," said the doctor. "So I would say you'll definitely be able to play the clarinet."

"Great!" said the patient. "Because I've always wanted to play the clarinet."

COPS AND RIBBERS

A Humorous Twist on the Beat of Life

STORE MANAGER: Why do you always pick my store to rob?
THIEF: You always advertise such great sales!

CALLER: Send the fire department, quick! There's a fire in my basement!
911 DISPATCHER: Did you throw water on it?
CALLER: Of course!
911 DISPATCHER: Well, there's no use in our coming then—that's all we ever do.

JUDGE: You look familiar . . . have we met before?
DEFENDANT: Yes—I taught your daughter to play the drums, remember?
JUDGE: Life in prison for you!

BOY: What happened to the guy who stole your dog?
GIRL: He was charged with pet-ty theft.

DEFENDANT: Your Honor, I'm not guilty of robbery. I'm a locksmith.

JUDGE: Well, what were you doing at the scene of the crime when the police arrived?

DEFENDANT: Just making a bolt for the door!

POLICEMAN: Why did you hit that tree?

DRIVER: Don't blame me! I honked at it but it wouldn't move.

TRAFFIC OFFICER: Did you know this is a one-way street?

DRIVER: Of course—I'm only driving one way!

What do you get when you cross a policeman with an alarm clock?

A crime watch.

What happened to the robber who stole the lamp?

Oh, he got a very light sentence.

What do you call a court case about swimwear?

A bathing suit.

Why was the artist arrested for graffiti?

He had to draw the line somewhere.

OKay, Van Gogh! Drop the crayons and turn around real slow...

Why did the cops arrest the baseball player?

They heard he had stolen third base.

How was the fish farm robbed?

By hook and by crook.

What do you call it when crooks go surfing?

A crime wave.

OK—Fins to the SKY, scale-face!

217

Did you hear about the crook at the scale factory?

Yeah, he got a weigh.

How did they catch the crooks at the pig farm?

Someone squealed.

Why didn't the police arrest the runner?

She had a good track record.

How did the robber get caught at the art gallery?

He was framed.

Why did the police investigate the seafood restaurant?
They knew something fishy was going on.

Why was the mime unhelpful in reporting the incident?
She couldn't say what had happened.

Why did the cops show up at the amusement park?
They heard somebody was being taken for a ride.

Why couldn't the judge convict the thief immediately?
You can't judge a crook by its cover.

What do you get when you cross a judge with poison ivy?
Rash decisions.

A writer was convicted of a terrible, bloody murder. After ten years in solitary confinement, he was brought before a judge to see if he felt remorse. "Do you feel sorry for what you did?" asked the judge. "Well, I . . ." replied the writer. After a moment, the writer was marched back to prison.

After twenty more years, the writer was a new man. He argued that he had given up his criminal ways for good, and applied for parole. "I can't let you go free," said the judge. "Why not?" asked the writer. "Well," said the judge, "you never finished your sentence." ☆

Amanda Bynes

A teenage girl with her very own TV show—impossible, you say? Just ask Amanda Bynes—she's got two! Amanda started performing at age seven at a kids' comedy camp. When a producer for Nickelodeon's show *All That* saw Amanda performing one night, he offered her an audition on the spot. *All That* features sketch comedy—short skits including familiar characters who act out funny situations—with frequent guest appearances of top music groups. Amanda's best-known character is Ashley, an advice columnist with some serious attitude. During her "Ask Ashley" segments, Amanda-as-Ashley screams at "dumb" letter writers so loudly that the actress frequently ends up with a sore throat!

The Amanda Show is Amanda's other gig. It's a variety show, mixing sketch comedy, celebrity guest spots, and musical acts—and, of course, it's named for its talented star! Amanda says she looks to *Saturday Night Live* for inspiration for her own show. She considers Lucille Ball and Bette Midler her comedic role models.

All in all, Amanda seems to be a pretty normal teenager—she likes Harry Potter and Beanie Babies, watches *Rugrats,* and sneaks bowls of sugared cereal whenever her dentist dad isn't around. She loves to shop and have sleepovers with her friends. While she admits that going to parties and meeting stars like Will Smith and Jim Carrey is a blast, she says, "I'm a regular kid . . . basically." Of her turn in showbiz, she says, "It's a different life, but it's a fantastic life. This is the life for me!"

Why couldn't the thunderclouds pull off the bank heist?

When the alarm went off, they all bolted.

Why was the comedian accused of assaulting his audience?

He gagged them and left them in stitches.

Why couldn't the cops catch the wallpaper thief?

There was a big cover-up.

How come the police didn't catch the man who robbed the Laundromat?

He made a clean getaway.

What did the paper police say to the rock criminal?

"You think your life's hard now? You just wait.
And don't think I don't know about your friend Scissors."

How did the runaway hairdresser escape from the police?

She knew all the short cuts.

220

What do you call it when someone crashes into a police officer?

A run-in with the law!

That's *him*! Yes—the big fat round guy in the center! He's the one!

What did the zero say when asked if he had committed the crime?

"I did nothing!"

COPS AND ROBBERS

BEHIND THE PUNCH LINE:
Hecklers

Stand-up comedy isn't always easy. Sometimes there are people in the audience called *hecklers* who don't think the comedian is funny or who don't think they're being entertained. A heckler will yell an insult at the comic, interrupting the monologue. A good comedian won't take the heckler seriously, and will yell something funny back, making everybody laugh. The best comedians will even get hecklers to laugh at themselves. The key is to stay cool—if you've rehearsed enough, then you won't be nervous—and play along. Improvisation techniques can be very helpful in dealing with hecklers. Take what they say and turn it into something funny. Your audience will think you're amazing!

221

How did the police know the blacksmith's signature was a fake?

It was forged.

Why didn't the police search for the missing rutabaga?

They knew it would turnip somewhere soon.

Why did the police raid the comic book store?

They were doing a strip search.

Why did the cops hang out at the coffee shop?

In case someone got mugged.

What do you get when you cross a SWAT team with an octopus?

A bomb squid.

What did the cops tell the mime when they arrested her?

"You still have the right to remain silent."

What did the police officer say when he caught the woman who had stolen the office equipment?

"Just give me the fax, ma'am."

Why were the charges against the football team dropped?

They had a strong defense.

How did the police know the photographer was guilty?

They found his prints all over the scene of the crime.

Did Sheriff Pat Garrett shoot Billy the Kid in the end?

No, he shot him right through the heart.

Thanksgiving Funnies:

Why were the Pilgrims' pants always falling down?
They wore their belts around their hats.

222

Ooh, that smarts!

The traffic cop pulls over a driver who has been speeding and asks him, "Didn't you see the speed limit signs posted on this road?"

"Why, officer," said the driver, "I was going much too fast to read those tiny little signs." ☆

Why did the cops plant catnip at the scene of the crime?
To catch a cat burglar.

223

JUDGE: Order in the court!
DEFENDANT: I'll have a cheeseburger and fries, Your Honor.

JUDGE: I find you guilty and I'm giving you a choice: fifteen thousand dollars or six months in jail.
DEFENDANT: Your Honor, I'll take the money!

POLICE OFFICER (putting handcuffs on a crook): If I were you, I'd get myself a good lawyer.
CROOK: Officer, if I could afford a good lawyer, I wouldn't have tried to rob that bank.

What do you get when you cross a bank robber with the Invisible Man?
You get away with it.

A police officer saw a woman sitting in her car with a tiger next to her. The officer said, "It's against the law to have that tiger in your car here on the street! Take him to the zoo."

The next day the police officer saw the same woman in the same car with the same tiger. He said, "I thought I told you to take that tiger to the zoo!"

The woman replied, "I did. He liked it so much, today we're going to the beach!" ☆

How did the mutt defend his crime?

He blamed it on bad breeding.

224

Why did the police officers arrest the python after the accident?

It was a hiss and run.

...no hands on the steering wheel, not wearing a seatbelt, and half of you is riding in the back seat!

HOW MANY ELEPHANTS...

Can You Fit in a Joke Book?

What happened to the elephant who had a nervous breakdown?

They had to give him trunquilizers.

Why do elephants have trunks?

Because they don't have glove compartments.

Why are elephants banned from public swimming pools?

They always drop their trunks.

Why are elephants so wrinkly?

They're too big to fit on the ironing board.

MAN: I'll bet you $100 that I can lift an elephant with one hand.
WOMAN: Ha! You're on!
MAN: Fine! Go find me an elephant with one hand!

"Waiter!" yells a customer. "What's this elephant doing in my bowl of alphabet soup?"

The waiter comes over and says, "I suppose he's learning to read." ✵

What's gray, has wings, and gives money to baby elephants?

The tusk fairy.

226

Hey- would you mind taking that hat off?

How do you know if there's an elephant in front of you at the movies?

You can't see the screen.

Why did the elephant paint himself brown?

So he could hide in the box of raisins.

What do you get when you cross an elephant with a kangaroo?

Big holes all over Australia.

Why did the elephant paint her toenails blue?

So she could hide in the blueberry bush.

PRACTICAL JOKE

How to avoid going to bed:

Wear plastic fangs and convince your parents that you're a vampire.

Explain that the country has recently gone on Daylight Super-Saving Time, so it's actually only four o'clock in the afternoon. (Warning: this will only work in the summer!)

Tell them that your science homework was to stay up and look for shooting stars, and that you'll flunk if you don't see at least one.

Insist that you must stand guard all night in order to finally get that monster in your closet.

Laugh and say, "I'm already in bed! You're just dreaming that I'm still awake!"

Explain that you are practicing for New Year's Eve and that you have to stay up all night long.

227

A man was walking by a restaurant when he saw a sign in the window that said, "We will pay $100 to anyone who orders something we can't make." The man went inside and sat down, and when the waitress came over he asked for an elephant sandwich. She dug in her apron, pulled out a roll of bills and handed the man $100.

"What's the matter?" he asked. "No elephants today?"

"Oh, we have elephants, all right," she answered. "We're just all out of the big buns." ✩

Why did the elephant paint himself red and white?

So he could hide in a can of Coca-Cola.

What do you call an elephant in a phone booth?

Stuck.

What's large, blue, and transparent on the outside?

An elephant stuck in a Ziploc bag.

228

What time is it when an elephant sits on a fence?

Time to get a new fence.

What's large, gray, and wears a trench coat?

An undercover elephant.

What's the difference between an elephant and a cookie?

Have you ever tried dunking an elephant in milk?

What did the elephant say when he walked into the post office?

"Ouch."

Why was the vacationing elephant so glum?

The airline lost his trunk.

Why do elephants have big trunks?

So they have somewhere to put the groceries when they go shopping.

What do you call an elephant on the run?

An earthquake.

Bill Cosby

Bill Cosby holds legendary status in the comedy world. He is a major force in the revival of wholesome family comedy. Cosby's popular sitcom *The Cosby Show*, which ran on NBC from 1984 to 1994, is credited with bringing funny family television back into style. The show, about a doctor, his lawyer wife, and their five kids, had episodes about things like report cards, curfews, and goldfish funerals—things every family could relate to.

Cosby has been a role model for African-Americans in entertainment since the 1960s, when he appeared on a detective show called *I Spy*. In the 1970s, Cosby created a cartoon show called *Fat Albert and the Cosby Kids* that was about young African-American kids growing up in the city. *The Cosby Show* and its spinoff (a show created with characters from the first program), *A Different World*, were praised for showing well-educated black characters in happy families. Cosby himself wrote several books about education and being a parent. His love for kids is evident in his most recent television hit, *Kids Say the Darndest Things*.

How do you wake up a sleeping elephant?

Use an alarm clock, silly.

How did Elton John get the elephant to play a duet?

He tickled her ivories.

What's the difference between a *Tyrannosaurus* rex and an elephant?

One dismembers; the other remembers.

What's the difference between a skateboard and an elephant?

One has four wheels; the other doesn't.

230

Where do you find an elephant?

Wherever you left her.

Why did the elephant leave the circus?

He was tired of working for peanuts.

Why don't elephants like elephant jokes?

They think they're Dumbo.

Where do elephants go to see art?

The peanut gallery.

You've hung this one upside down!

What's the difference between an elephant and a loaf of bread?

If you don't know, then let's hope no one ever sends you to the corner store to buy a loaf of bread!

Why did the elephant forget?

She didn't renew her remembership.

231

How many elephants can you see on a clear night?

It depends where you're standing.

What do you call it when an elephant runs into two other elephants?

A three-squealer.

What's small and pink?

An elephant's tutu.

What's old, gray, and wrinkled?

A stale raisin pretending to be an elephant.

What do you get when you cross a ghost with an elephant?

Wrinkled sheets.

THE MAKING OF A COMEDIAN

Step 7: Don't Give It All Away!

Shhhh! We didn't just give these jokes away, did we? Well, neither should you. Never, ever blurt out a punch line before its time. You shouldn't ask people if they've heard the joke before, because you might give yourself away in the process. A funny joke is like a well-planned surprise party—the bigger the surprise, the happier the party.

232

What should an elephant bring to a ballet audition?

Her own ballet shoes.

How do you make an elephant laugh?

Tickle him.

What should you do for an elephant with an upset stomach?

Stay as far away from her as possible.

What should you do when an elephant drives you up the wall?

Take away his license.

What's an elephant's favorite card game?

Memory.

What should you do with an elephant in a cast?

Make sure she knows her lines.

What should you do about an elephant who is attacking you along with a *Tyrannosaurus rex* and a man-eating saber-toothed tiger?

The elephant is the least of your worries. It eats only plants.

What's large, gray, and goes up and down?

An elephant in an exercise class.

What's large, gray, and hard to spot?

A stain-resistant elephant.

Why do elephants drive Volkswagens?

There's room for four and the rest is trunk space.

How can you tell if there's an elephant in your bag of Oreos?

Read the list of ingredients.

233

How do you know there's an elephant in the bottom of your bunk bed?

Your nose touches the ceiling.

How can you tell when there are two elephants in your refrigerator?

You can hear them giggling.

SNORE...

Why are elephants known to hold grudges?

They can forgive, but they can't forget.

So, YOU'RE the doctor who slapped me when I was born!

How can you tell when there are three elephants in your refrigerator?

Open the refrigerator door and check, silly.

234

How can you tell if there are four elephants in your refrigerator?

The light is on and there's a Volkswagen parked outside.

Why do elephants wear sneakers?

So they can sneak up on peanuts.

Why don't elephants like computers?

They're afraid of the mouse.

What do you call an elephant on a bike?

Wheelie dangerous.

Why did the elephant go running?

It wanted to jog its memory.

How do you stop an elephant from charging?

Take away his credit card!

Knock, knock.
Who's there?
Gladys.
Gladys who?
Gladys you and not another elephant joke!

MONSTER-OSITIES

Ghouls, Goblins, and the Like

What do you get when alien teenagers invade shopping malls on Earth?

Clothes encounters of the third kind.

What should you do to keep a corpse from smelling?

Nothing, silly, dead people can't smell!

Did you hear the one about the vampire?

It was a vein attempt at humor.

What kind of telephones do mummies use?

Touch-tomb phones.

Once upon a time a rich dumb king had a beautiful daughter named Molly. One day a fierce dragon came by and carried Molly off into his cave high on a mountain top. "Just wait a minute, mister," said Molly. "Dragons aren't real. Here, I'll show you." And she pulled a pocket encyclopedia out of her purse.

The dragon put on his reading glasses. "Hmm . . . Aardvarks, abalones, beavers . . . gazelles, gryphons . . . unicorns, vultures . . . zebras, zebus, zombies. Nope, no dragons." And the dragon instantly disappeared.

"How did you escape from that horrible dragon?" the king asked Molly.

"Easy. I proved to him that dragons don't exist. Now are you or aren't you going to buy me that pet unicorn for my birthday?" ✩

236

What's a werewolf's favorite day of the week?

Moonday.

Two dragons are chasing a knight in armor. Just as they are about to catch him, the first dragon says, "You remembered to bring the barbecue sauce this time, right?"

The second dragon answers, "Yes. And I hope you remembered the can opener." ✩

Okay, stay right there while I get the salad...

LITTLE GHOUL: No fair! Why can you go to the Halloween party and I can't?

BIG GHOUL: Because I'm the mummy, that's why!

Did you hear about the two mind readers who met on the street?

The first one said, "Well, you're fine. How am I?"

What kind of TV do you find in a haunted house?

A big-scream TV.

At what time did Dracula go to the dentist?

Tooth hurty.

Did you hear the one about the mummies?

Too bad, it wrapped already.

BAD JOKE BREAK

Exasperate a friend! You say the lines in bold; the lines after the bold lines are answers your friend will most likely give. The most important thing about this trick is to go on long enough so that your friend is confident with her answers. Then you make her groan when you get to the trick at the end!

What's red and goes "ding dong"?

I don't know—what?

A red ding dong. What's blue and goes "ding dong"?

A blue ding dong?

Right! What's green and goes "ding dong"?

A green ding dong?

Right again. Now, what's purple and goes "ding dong?"

Why, that must be a purple ding dong.

Correct. And what's pink and goes "ding dong"?

A pink ding dong?

Nope. They don't come in pink.

237

What do you say if the Abominable Snowman is about to chomp your head off?

"Chill, dude."

Why is it good to tell ghost stories in hot weather?

Because they are so chilling.

What do squirrels say on Halloween?

Trick or tree.

238

What does Tweety Bird say on Halloween?

Twick or tweet.

BOY: I'll stop being frightened if you'll stop being scared.
GIRL: That sounds like a fear trade to me.

BOY: Daddy, when were you in Egypt?
FATHER: Egypt? I was never in Egypt.
BOY: Then where did you get my mummy?

What do 18-wheelers say on Halloween?

Truck or treat.

What do diplomats say on Halloween?

Trick or treaty.

R.L. Stine and the Goosebumps

Robert Lawrence (R. L. to his fans) Stine, the author of the wildly popular series *Goosebumps,* began writing stories when he was nine years old. An avid comic book reader as a kid, he especially enjoyed the scary ones like *Tales from the Crypt* and *Vault of Horror.* Stine says those comic books strongly influenced the writing in his own scary stories. "When I write, I try to think back to what I was afraid of or what was scary to me, and try to put those feelings into books," he says. *Goosebumps* is also a poplar TV show on the Fox network. A movie might be next!

Stine once edited a joke magazine called *Bananas* under the name Jovial Bob. As Jovial Bob, he also wrote several joke books, including *101 Silly Monster Jokes* and *Bozos on Patrol.* He says his background as a funnyman helps him because he knows what will make kids laugh as well as what will scare them. This sixth sense for kids' book tastes has earned him the nickname "the children's Stephen King." Combining giggles with ghouls makes *Goosebumps* that much more enjoyable! In fact, Stine says the best way to be a writer of any kind is to have a broad reading background. After all, the more you read, the more things you know about that you can write about!

A woman was driving to the grocery store one day when suddenly there was a puff of smoke in the passenger seat. A little red man with a tail materialized. When the smoke finally cleared, he spoke up. "Hello," said the little red man. "Why don't you try running through this red light?"

"I don't think that's a good idea," answered the woman angrily. She waited for the green, and continued driving down the street. Soon, she got stuck behind a slow truck.

"Bet you can't step on the gas and pass him," coaxed the little red man.

"Will you stop telling me how to drive?" the woman said in a huff.

"What are you, chicken?" the little red man said with a grin.

The woman turned to the little red man and looked at him suspiciously. "Wait a second," she said. "Are you Satan, the King of Evil?"

"No," the little man replied, "I'm just a daredevil."

240

I'm savink zis for a suhny day...

Where did the vampire open his savings account?

At the blood bank.

Did you hear about the poor vampire slayer?
He tried to kill a vampire by driving a pork chop through its heart because steaks were too expensive.

Why didn't the skeleton cross the road?
Because he didn't have the guts.

Why don't witches ride on their brooms when they're angry?

What does a ghost eat for lunch?

A boo-logna sandwich.

What did the mommy ghost say to the baby ghost?

Don't spook until you're spooken to.

How do vampires get around on Halloween night?

By blood vessels.

Why do ghouls and demons hang out together?

Because demons are a ghoul's best friend.

What happened to the guy who couldn't keep up on the payments to his exorcist?

He was re-possessed.

What is Transylvania?

Dracula's terror-tory.

Why should a skeleton drink lots of milk?

It's good for the bones.

Where do mummies go for a swim?

The Dead Sea.

They're afraid of flying off the handle.

Where does Dracula water ski?

On Lake Eerie.

Who won the skeleton beauty contest?

No body.

What do skeletons say before they start to eat?

"Bone appetit!"

Where do baby ghosts go during the day?

To a dayscare center.

242

Why are most monsters covered in wrinkles?

Have you ever tried to iron a monster?

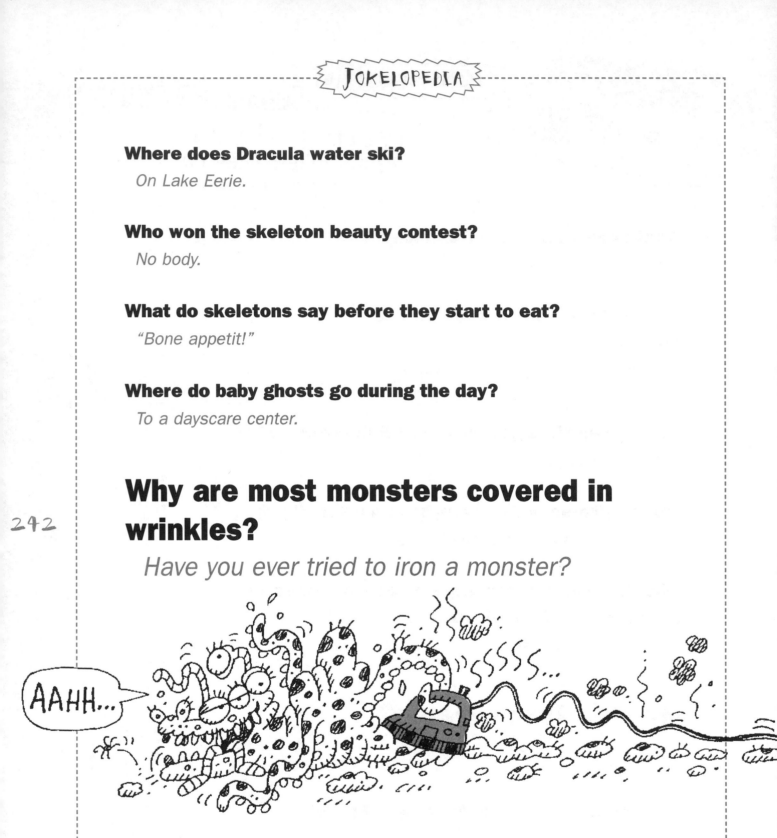

AAHH...

Who did Frankenstein take to the prom?

His ghoul friend.

What do ghosts serve for dessert?

Ice scream.

What's a monster's favorite play?

Romeo and Ghouliet.

What do witches put in their hair?

Scare spray.

What do you get when you cross Bambi with a ghost?

Bamboo.

What do you call a haunted chicken?

A poultry-geist.

What kind of mistakes do ghosts make?

Boo boos.

Why do mummies make excellent spies?

They're good at keeping things under wraps.

What kind of monster is safe to put in the washing machine?

A wash-and-wear wolf.

What do you call a person who puts poison in someone's corn flakes?

A cereal killer.

How did the ghost fix the hole in his sheet?

With a pumpkin patch.

What is the largest building in Transylvania?

The Vampire State Building.

Eye of Newt makes great sunscreen!

What would you find on a haunted beach?

A sand witch.

What do goblins and ghosts drink when they're hot and thirsty?

Ghoul-Aid.

What is a vampire's favorite holiday?

Fangsgiving.

What's it like to be kissed by a vampire?

It's a pain in the neck.

A monster is devouring an entire football team. Another monster comes along and argues that he's eating more than his share. "Okay," the first monster says. "I'll give you halfback."

Why don't mummies take vacations?

They're afraid they'll relax and unwind.

What would you get if you crossed a spaniel, a French poodle, a ghost, and a rooster?

A cocker-poodle-boo!

When do ghosts usually appear?

Just before someone screams.

244

Addams Family

The mysterious and spooky, altogether ooky Addams family began as a series of cartoons drawn by Charles Addams for *The New Yorker* magazine from 1932 until his death in 1988. In the early 1960s, a TV producer decided to create a show based on Addams's drawings. The main characters were Gomez and Morticla Addams; their children, Puggsley and Wednesday; Uncle Fester; Lurch, the butler; and lovable Cousin Itt. In 1991, a movie called *The Addams Family* came out, followed by a sequel, *Addams Family Values,* in 1993. The movies introduced Addams's characters to a whole new generation, along with the familiar theme song (snap, snap). The appeal of the Addams family was that they didn't seem to realize their own freakiness—making their encounters with the world outside their creepy mansion (with its own graveyard) all the funnier. Remember little Wednesday in the first film, asking whether the Girl Scout cookies contained real Girl Scouts?

What do you call the ghost of a door-to-door salesperson?

A dead ringer.

Why do dragons sleep during the day?

So they can fight knights.

Why do witches think they're funny?

Every time they look in the mirror, it cracks up.

How do you make a strawberry shake?

Sneak up behind it and yell "BOO!"

246

What happens when a flying witch breaks the sound barrier?

You hear the broom boom.

Why did the other kids have to let the vampire play baseball?

It was his bat.

What has a broom and flies?

A jelly-covered janitor.

What do you get when you cross a monster with a cat?

A mew-tation.

How do mummies hide?

They wear masking tape.

What kind of dog does Dracula have?

A bloodhound.

Where does Count Dracula wash his hair?

In the bat tub.

Knock, knock.
Who's there?
Avon.
Avon who?
Avon to suck your blood.

Why did the vampire's girlfriend dump him?

The relationship was too draining.

247

Why did Count Dracula see his doctor?

He was always coffin.

Why did the vampire run screaming out of the restaurant?

He found out it was a stake house.

What do you call a bloodthirsty Philadelphian?

A Pennsylvanian Transylvanian.

Where do you store a werewolf?

In a were-house.

What kind of fur do you get from a werewolf?

As fur away as possible.

What should you do when you find a ghost in your living room?

Offer him a sheet.

What should you do with overweight ghosts?

Exorcize them.

Knock, knock.
Who's there?
Voodoo.
Voodoo who?
Voodoo you think you are?

How do ghosts get to school in the morning?

They take a ghoul bus.

What do ghost babies wear on their feet?

Boo-tees!

How does a monster count to 142?

On its fingers.

Why wasn't the girl afraid of the monster?

It was a man-eating monster.

What's pink and soft and found between a monster's teeth?

Slow runners.

A group of Boy Scouts and their leader were walking through a forest one day. They found their campsite and began to pitch their tents. There were ten boys, and each one had a tent, so it took a long time. Once they were finished, they lit a campfire. They roasted marshmallows over the fire and sang songs until it was very late at night. Each boy went into his own tent and into his own sleeping bag. At about two o'clock in the morning, there was a rustle in the bushes. The boys and their leader all woke up. Each one got out of his sleeping bag and then out of his tent to see what was making the noise. Once outside, the Boy Scouts found a large purple-spotted monster with ten arms. The boys tried to run away, but each of the purple-spotted monster's arms caught one boy. The monster quickly gobbled up all the Scouts it had caught. The Boy Scout leader watched in horror because there was nothing he could do. He ran away as quickly as he could. He ran through the forest and all the way back to the Boy Scout base. When he got there, he was completely out of breath. The other leaders looked at him and asked what was wrong.

"Well, we set up camp as usual. Then, in the middle of the night, we heard a rustle. When we got out of our tents to see what it was, we found a purple-spotted monster. The monster had ten arms and caught all ten boys. It gobbled them up and there was nothing I could do."

"You must be lying. Tell us where the Scouts really are."

"I'm not lying: that was the whole troop and nothing but the troop." ☆

249

Does this mean I get my purple-spotted monster merit badge?

Why don't monsters eat clowns?

They taste funny.

What do you call a giant monster who lives in the ocean and makes loud noises when he drinks?

A sea slurpant.

What giant monster lives in the mountains and hems men's suits?

The abominable sew-man.

250

Why don't abominable snowmen ever marry?

They always get cold feet.

What do you call a large gorilla who likes to dance?

King Conga.

We dare you to try this spooky, slippery tongue twister three times fast:

Which witch watched which witch's watch walk?

Why did the ghoul cry when her pet zombie ran away?

Because he ran off with her mummy.

Why couldn't the young witch find a job?

She didn't have enough hex-perience.

How can you tell when two monsters are getting along?

Why did the wizard drop out of school?

He couldn't spell.

Why didn't the two four-eyed monsters marry?

Because they could never see eye to eye to eye to eye.

Why did the little skeleton feel left out?

He had no body to play with.

251

Why don't skeletons go bungee jumping?

Because they don't have any guts.

How did Frankenstein know he was in love?

He felt that certain spark.

Why did the Blob stay home on Saturday night?

He was all dressed up with nowhere to goo.

They see eye to eye to eye to eye to
eye to eye to eye to eye.

A vampire bat came flapping in from the night covered in fresh blood, and parked himself on the roof of the cave to get some sleep. Pretty soon all the other bats smelled the blood and began asking him where he got it. He told them to knock it off and let him get some sleep, but they persisted until finally he gave in. "OK, follow me," he said, and flew out of the cave with hundreds of bats behind him. Down through a valley they went, across a river, and into a forest full of trees. Finally he slowed down and all the other bats excitedly milled around him. "Now, do you see that tree over there?" he asked. "Yes, yes, yes!" the bats all screamed in a frenzy. "Good," said the first bat. "Because *I didn't!*"

Why did Godzilla visit New York on Saturday evening?

He wanted a night out on the town.

Say-these taste great! Crunchy with a creamy filling!

REALLY OLD JOKES

Extinct Animals and Funny Fossils

Where did *Tyrannosaurus rex* live?

Anywhere it wanted to.

What gets wetter and wetter the more it dries?

A towel.

Why aren't there any dinosaurs in animal crackers?

Because they're extinct, silly! And anyway, they don't fit in the box.

What would you get if you crossed a dinosaur with a pig?

Jurassic Pork.

An old man got up every morning at six o'clock to sprinkle white powder on his front and back yards. One morning his paper boy asked him: "Why are you always putting powder around your house?"

"To keep the dinosaurs away," replied the old man.

"But there aren't any dinosaurs left," said the little boy.

"Well, then, it worked!" said the old man. ✦

Did you hear the rumor about the dinosaur that terrorized Florida?
It was a croc.

How do you know when a dinosaur has gone bad?
Check her expiration date.

What do you get when you cross a prehistoric animal with a cat?
A 'saur puss.

254

THUN-KA THUN-KA THUN-KA THUN-KA

What music do hip dinosaurs listen to?
Raptor music.

What's the difference between a pterodactyl and a chicken?
When you come down with a cold, nobody ever offers you a bowl of hot pterodactyl soup.

What's the difference between a pterodactyl and a turkey?

The drumsticks are bigger on a pterodactyl.

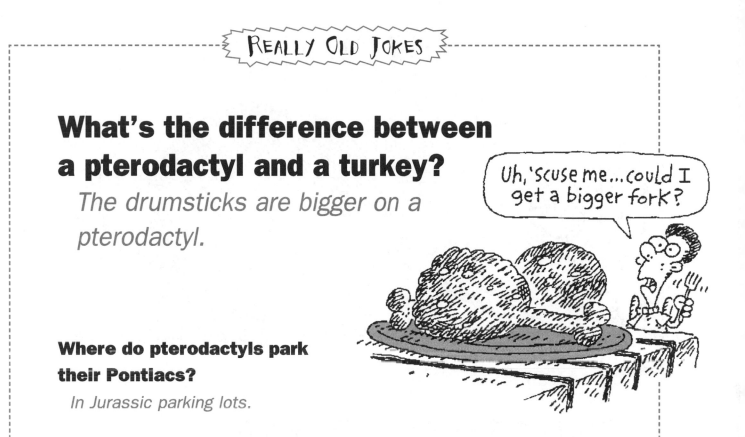

Uh, 'scuse me...could I get a bigger fork?

Where do pterodactyls park their Pontiacs?

In Jurassic parking lots.

What's the difference between a pterodactyl and a parrot?

You'd know the answer if you ever let a pterodactyl sit on your shoulder.

255

Who puts braces on woolly mammoths?

The mastodontist.

Why did the brontosaurus climb into the active volcano?

He wasn't very smart.

What did the stegosaurus say to the cute brontosaurus at the tar pit?

"Hey, I'm glad you decided to stick around."

256

How do you know there's a brontosaurus in the house?

The cheese is missing from the mousetraps.

How do you know there's a tyrannosaurus in the house?

The brontosaurus is missing.

What do you call it when a tyrannosaurus throws a brontosaurus at another tyrannosaurus?

Food fight!

Where did the dodo bird like to fly for his winter vacation?

Nowhere—dodoes couldn't fly.

Why did the first fish grow legs and walk out of the ocean?

He had to go to the bathroom.

BEHIND THE PUNCH LINE:

Classic Comedy

Good comedy is all about pleasing the audience. Take William Shakespeare, for example. Usually, we think of Shakespeare's plays as difficult academic works. But in the language of his time, Shakespeare's comedic plays, such as *The Taming of the Shrew*, *As You Like It*, and *Twelfth Night*, were uproariously funny and loaded with plays on words, silly characters, and loads of comic situations. The playwright's tragedies were masterpieces of the English language, too. Many of our sayings come directly from Shakespeare, in fact. Shakespeare wrote for the people—he consciously avoided the stiff, snobby style of other writers in order to please the people in the theater.

257

When did cave people invent hockey?

During the ice age.

If a triceratops and a pebble are standing on the edge of a cliff, which one jumps first?

The pebble—it's a little boulder.

What should you do if a grizzly bear gets caught in the trap you set for a *Tyrannosaurus rex*?

Let it go. Grizzly bears are an endangered species.

How do you know if there's a triceratops under your bed?

You listen for a dino-snore.

Which dinosaur roamed the wild, wild west?

Tyrannosaurus Tex.

And what did he ride?

A bronco-saurus.

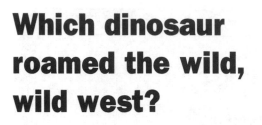

258

William says to Gillian one day, "Your dad seems to get along well with your pet *Tyrannosaurus rex*. I guess that's because no one would want to argue with twelve tons of unstoppable fury."

Gillian says, "Hey, watch it, that's my dad you're talking about!"

How do you brush a saber-toothed tiger's teeth?

Very carefully.

What's Barney's favorite movie?

The Color Purple.

What's louder than a dinosaur?

A whole bunch of dinosaurs.

What do you get when you turn a dinosaur upside down?

A triceratops-y turvy.

One day, a stegosaurus decided to go for a walk. The stegosaurus walked up a mountain, down a road, and through a valley. At one end of the valley, it met another stegosaurus.

The other stegosaurus wanted some company, so it followed the first stegosaurus back across the valley, up the road, and down the other side of the mountain. There they met a third stegosaurus. The third stegosaurus was also lonely and so it followed the other two stegosauruses.

They walked down another road and through another valley and up a small hill. There they met another stegosaurus who was lonely and so decided to join the other three. All four stegosauruses headed off together and walked back up the small hill and through the other valley. This time they took a right turn and headed down a new road, which ended in a forest. There they met another stegosaurus having lunch.

What did the stegosaurus say when it saw the other four?

Nothing. Stegosauruses can't talk. ☆

259

What do you call a reptile who hangs out in sleazy bars?
A lounge lizard.

What's round, covered with chocolate, and tastes like a wooly mammoth?
A masto-donut.

KNOCK-KNOCKS

Knock, knock.

Who's there?

Jurassic.

Jurassic who?

Jurassic person if you think this joke is funny!

———

Knock, knock.

Who's there?

Police.

Police who?

Po-lice open the door!

———

Knock, knock.

Who's there?

Deluxe.

Deluxe who?

Deluxe-smith. I'm here to fix de lock.

———

Knock, knock.

Who's there?

Polo.

Polo who?

Polo-ver, you're under arrest.

———

Knock, knock.

Who's there?

Xena.

Xena who?

Xena good movie lately?

Knock, knock.

Who's there?

Anita.

Anita who?

Anita nother minute to think it over.

———

Knock, knock.

Who's there?

Electra.

Electra who?

Electricity. Isn't that shocking?

———

Knock, knock.

Who's there?

Omelette.

Omelette who?

Omelette smarter than I sound.

———

Knock, knock.

Who's there?

Thor.

Thor who?

Thorry, wrong door.

———

Knock, knock.

Who's there?

IBM.

IBM who?

IBM. Who be you?

260

Knock, knock.
Who's there?
Raven.
Raven who?
Raven lunatic who wants to knock your door down!

Knock, knock.
Who's there?
Sparrow.
Sparrow who?
Sparrow me the details and let me in.

Knock, knock.
Who's there?
Huron.
Huron who?
Huron my toe, could you please step off it?

———

Knock, knock.
Who's there?
Lotus.
Lotus who?
Lotus in and we'll tell you.

———

Knock, knock.
Who's there?
Comma.
Comma who?
Comma little closer and I'll kiss you.

———

Knock, knock.
Who's there?
Alaska.
Alaska who?
Alaska 'nother person if you don't know the answer.

Knock, knock.
Who's there?
Wire.
Wire who?
Wire you asking me that again. I just told you!

———

Knock, knock.
Who's there?
Byte.
Byte who?
Byte you're happy to see me again.

———

Knock, knock.
Who's there?
DOS.
DOS who?
DOS your computer have an operating system?

261

Knock, knock.
Who's there?
Cow go.
Cow go who?
No, cow go moo.

TONGUE TWISTERS

Try these totally tasteless tongue twisters:

Sick Suzy sucks slimy snot.

Can canned clams can clams?

The fifth fink sinks faster than the first four finks think.

Such a silly tongue twister mustn't be mumbled.

Feeble felines fear fur.

Sneaking in my creaky squeaky reeking sneakers.

Bee stings sting severely when it's sunburned skin that's stung.

I'm hooked on the book Brooke brought back from the Brookside bookstore.

Kent sent Trent the rent to rent Trent's tent.

Sally saw Shelley singing swinging summer swimming songs.

The corn on the cob made Bob the Slob's sobbing stop.

The ocean sure soaked Sherman.

Can you say these three times fast?

She freed six sick sheep.

She freed three shy sheep.

FREE
THE
SICK
SIX

RECORD YOUR OWN JOKES

263

RECORD YOUR OWN JOKES